SHARPER THAN ANY TWO-EDGED SWORD

BY

WARREN HARDIG

For the word of God is living and active, and sharper than any two-edged sword, even penetrating as far as the division of soul and spirit, of both joints and marrow, and able to judge the thoughts and intentions of the heart.
Hebrews 4:12

First paperback edition May, 2022.

Cover design by Larry Taylor.

ISBN 978-1-8803-3858-2

Other books by Warren Hardig
Iron Sharpens Iron
Still Sharpening

This book is dedicated to the men who came before me:
my father Woodrow and father-in-law George

and the ones who are coming behind me:
my beloved son Roger, son-in-law Steve,
and grandsons Ben and Elijah.

With special love and recognition to Velma,
my precious wife and sidearm

and to Reneé,
my daughter who is the delight of my heart.

ACKNOWLEDGMENTS

This book is about Jesus and what He can do through the life of an ordinary layman who has made Christ the lord of his life. The organization Men for Missions Global, formerly Men for Missions International, is usually referred to as MFM or Men for Missions, a movement born of God.

I thank the Lord for every person named in this book. It is an honor and a privilege to call each one a friend. I am fortunate to have a multitude of friends around the world who, if their stories were in print, would bless and encourage you. I have spent most of the last 48 years challenging men and their families to surrender to Jesus and telling them about Men for Missions; that is what this book focuses on.

Whatever good has come from my life is because of Jesus and having a wife as described in Proverbs 31:11-12. Our children, Roger and Reneé, have benefited from meeting the myriad of people who paraded through our homes who loved and encouraged them to be the godly people they are today, knowing they were children of kingdom-focused parents.

Then there is the edit team of Clance LaTurner and Buddy Balogh who, along with Velma, have the final word on what goes to the printer. Judy Evans put in print a lot of my handwritten notes. Mykaela Alvey picked up any ball she was thrown and carried it well. I am forever grateful to our team of readers – David Dick, Frieda Dowler, Hilda Duewel, David Dunstan, Ann Gipson, Kent Eller, Karine McLaughlin, Carroll Rader, Jim Slone, Jim Turnbull and Carolyn Watts – who invested in polishing and placement. Clance has coordinated this effort with excellence.

"Not to us, oh Lord, not to us, but to Your name give glory because of Your lovingkindness, because of Your truth" (Psalm 115:1). The entire team joins with me to give God the glory for each word, and prays you are drawn closer to Him by what you read.

TABLE OF CONTENTS

Introduction
Sharper Than Any Two-Edged Sword

The theme of this book is the sharpness of the true and living Word of God: "For the Word of God is living and active and sharper than any two-edged sword" (Hebrews 4:12). It continues the theme of *Iron Sharpens Iron* and *Still Sharpening,* with the testimonies of some of my friends from varied countries and cultures. The Word of God and His Holy Spirit convict us of sin and clothe us in righteousness, assuring us of God's forgiveness through His Son Jesus Christ.

I cannot tell you exactly what chapter I was reading on Monday, May 6, 1968. I do know I was reading God's word, with a cigarette in one hand and a cup of coffee in the other, when a clear voice asked me, "Why are you still smoking when you have a wife and a preacher who are praying for you?"

I went to the corner station and bought a pack of cigarettes then drove through the country to the farm chemical business I managed for Standard Oil of Indiana. There I knelt down at a chair in my office to pray. "God, I don't have to tell you I am a sinner. You know that better than anyone else. Would you forgive me of my sins so I can be a Christian? Would you take these cigarettes from me? We both know I can't quit in my own strength. Would you give me your Holy Spirit?" I continued to pray for another five or ten minutes.

When I stood to my feet, I felt like my soul had had a bath! My first thought was, *Why hasn't someone told me about this?* For ten years I had habitually chain smoked at least three packs of cigarettes a day; that day I experienced an instant deliverance from tobacco. Even the previous day I had smoked five packs, but now everything had changed.

That night I called the preacher and told him what God had done in my heart and life. I began to read the Word every morning. My day started at 3:30 a.m., and I spent two hours praying and reading the Word. Thanks to the strength and ability God gave me, I could navigate my growing faith while working six 20-hour days in the chemical business.

The saturation of the Word excited me about providing Bibles in closed countries. Our brothers and sisters who have the Word of God have greater strength to fight the enemy. “He who gives attention to the Word will find good, and blessed is he who trusts in the Lord” (Proverbs 16:20).

Those who have never read the Word don’t know what they have missed. Years ago, a friend of mine in Manila told me about his being “marinated in the Word.” I use this phrase “marinated in the Word” to describe the most desirable way to live.

One of the benefits of the Gospel for me is to see how it has changed the lives of individuals from almost every continent. God changes lives on dirt floors in Third World countries (the world’s most underdeveloped, poverty-stricken, and marginalized regions of the world), on jet airplanes flying over the Pacific Ocean, and on street corners in cities and towns all over the world. God shows His mercy in every corner of the world.

When my wife Velma and I moved to Greenwood, Indiana, we began to meet new people such as Harry and Eleanor Burr, leaders in One Mission Society (OMS) who were highly respected in Greenwood and around the world. Being friends and coworkers with the Burrs carried us into new social circles.

The Burrs introduced us to Paul Totten, a World War II veteran and local city council member who was instrumental in approving the

Oriental Missionary Society's move from California to 941 Fry Road in Indiana. It was a controversial move to allow an organization with "Oriental" in its name to move to conservative Greenwood, and it stimulated many protests from the missionaries who did not want to leave California and relocate to the Midwest.

Paul worked as a businessman and respected community leader in his hometown. Beyond that, he was a very highly decorated war hero who quietly said, "I am no hero."

Paul always dressed in a conservative wardrobe, presented himself clean shaven, and greeted you with a warm smile and firm handshake. He was soft spoken, never raised his voice, and drew you in with his smile.

He impressed me as a man who would never even throw the neighbor's cat out of his yard, much less one who received two Bronze Stars in combat. He fought in the jungles of the South Pacific for months without a bath, change of clothes, toothbrush, or other toiletries. As a prisoner of war, he was brutally beaten in a combat zone where many American comrades fought.

There is a park in the Philippines named for Paul, where he helped dispel the enemy in a confrontation. In recent years, Paul was honored by the Greenwood Rotary. Loren Minnix, a local businessman and friend to us all, read excerpts from a book written about Paul at one of our meetings; it gave us graphic details. Afterward there was a question-and-answer time. During a lull in questions, Paul shared the question he is most frequently asked, "Do you hate the Japanese?"

He said his standard answer has always been, "No, I love everybody. Gene Bertolet led me to a personal relationship with Jesus Christ. My life has changed."

The war we fight is not against flesh and blood but against the forces of evil. Paul is now in heaven enjoying our Lord, leaving behind a wall full of medals for his heroism.

Paul suggested the name of this book to me from Hebrews 4:12, "For the Word of God is living and active and sharper than any two-edged sword." Though I'm a reluctant author, I'm excited about this book since he gave the gift of that verse to me. Even though Paul isn't physically with us as we see this through to fruition, I know he is leaning over the banister of heaven tenderly watching everyone who reads *Sharper Than Any Two-Edged Sword.*

Through Men for Missions, a myriad of men have experienced their life-changing journeys in many different countries. Through Men for Missions, I experienced a dramatic change in my value system. Through Men for Missions, I'm blessed with many wonderful friends and amazing experiences; however, my main goal, and the goal of Men for Missions, is to glorify God.

"Not to us, oh Lord, not to us, but to Your name give glory because of Your lovingkindness, because of Your truth" (Psalm 115:1).

Author's notes:

When I asked these men to share their stories, I did not specify any word count. Each man responded in kind, sharing from his heart. I trust you will enjoy and be inspired by the stories that follow my brief introduction of each author, regardless of the length.

Also, there is a Glossary of Terms in the back of the book, in case you come across unfamiliar terms.

Items marked with an asterisk* throughout the book indicate descriptions that are listed in the Glossary of Terms.

-Warren

Broken Heart Club

Warren Hardig

"Those who sow in tears shall reap with joyful shouting" (Psalm 126:5).

The two greatest needs in the church today are prayer and people who will spread the Good News. Few people seem to know how to tell others about how Jesus changed them and gave them the assurance of eternal life. There can be nothing more precious in our lives than to know Christ, and to know our sins are forgiven.

I believe the most important question any of us should be able to answer is: *What will happen when you die?* It is imperative that we ask those around us this same question, spurring them on to consider their eternal fate. Eternal life is a promise Jesus has given us. We don't have to simply hope; we know. We are told, "I go and prepare a place for you, I will come again and receive you to Myself, that where I am, you may be also" (John 14:3 NKJV).

John Piper said, "The number one reason why prayer malfunctions in the hands of believers is that they try to turn a wartime walkie-talkie into a domestic intercom." (John Piper, Prayer: The Work of Missions, from *Desiring God*). We are literally in spiritual warfare and must learn to fight well, staying on our knees in prayer.

The fire of Dwight Ferguson and his preaching spiritually changed much if not all of southern Illinois for many years, and there is still a remnant of the fire in second and third generations of people. Dwight was fearless in his attack on the gates of hell as he ministered to people in the oil fields, restaurants, and churches across the tip of the state. No domestic intercom for Dwight. The Gospel of Jesus Christ he so boldly proclaimed showed multitudes of people their need for Christ. Jesus lit a fire in the hearts of many people, changing the local churches, Men for Missions, and the Oriental Missionary Society. I am one of those changed men.

My wife Velma and I were launched into the world by what we call the "Broken Heart Club." Our introduction to what was then called the Oriental Missionary Society was at a prayer meeting in southeastern Illinois. The emphasis was on holiness and prayer. Total obedience to Christ was a standard, and it was about the whole family. The last Saturday night of the month a few of us drove 50 miles to a host home to pray. Approximately 40 to 50 adults plus their children attended the meeting. We were a unique group. Some of us were young with small children, while others were not so young. Our group had retirees, a banker, farmers, schoolteachers, businessmen and housewives, all in love with Jesus Christ and wanting the ends of the earth to know Him.

We received packets of OMS missionaries' prayer letters, which we read and prayed over. Velma and I knew two of the couples fairly well; the rest we came to love as we stayed on our knees with them. We prayed from different social statuses and locations, and most of us at different times would weep over what we read. These beloved missionaries were facing challenges with enemy strongholds, children not understanding why they were there, diseases, projects that needed funding, sin taking its toll in the church, and many other issues. These folks cared so much for the missionaries and their work that they cried; we truly were in a Broken Heart Club.

MFM/Broken Heart Club Picnic in West Salem, IL, circa 1975.

I have been asked numerous times, "Who started the OMS prayer group that you named the Broken Heart Club?" Well, I really don't know, except to say it included friends who had been touched by Dwight Ferguson and other OMS missionaries. The emphasis was holiness and prayer. Total obedience to Christ, as well as concern for the whole family. In addition to our monthly meetings and annual events, the OMS Annual Conference was a big deal that everyone did their level best to attend for fresh inspiration.

The Broken Heart Club still has some members carrying people, including us, to the throne of God in prayer. Others joined OMS or MFM as career missionaries. Many are in heaven.

What about the results of the Broken Heart Club, now that many are in heaven? Before going home to be with Jesus, they passed their mantles on to their children and grandchildren. Through the years, the people of several generations have helped build churches, schools, and other needed structures. They provided a generator for Radio 4VEH in Cap-Haitien, overhauled many missionaries' cars, and purchased several new cars and trucks for missions work in the U.S. and Japan. Monuments to their love and obedience are all over the world, from bridges to entire universities. I was privileged to drive cars provided by the Broken Heart Club for several years while I was a regional director with Men for Missions. Those dear folks carried me in their cars and prayers for an average of 65,000 miles a year.

Once I went to Ecuador for a month of evangelism, leaving Velma, Roger, and Reneé at home in West Liberty, Illinois; our washer quit, and the men and women of the Broken Heart Club bought a new one and installed it. They also transported countless tons of missionary freight in their farm trucks over the years, which eased the financial burden of the missionaries as they left for their assigned fields of ministry.

When Roger was three, we were meeting one evening in the home of Bob Bruce in Fairfield, Illinois. This was in the days before cell phones, so we rarely had any distractions. However, Bruce's telephone rang that evening, and it was for me. I knew immediately it was bad news. Sure enough, the other end of the line was Emma, Velma's mother, with news that Velma's aunt and uncle had been killed in an explosion that destroyed their two-story farm home. Earlier that day the company that furnished gas which would heat their home installed a new storage tank, which caused a seal in the gas line to malfunction, triggering a leak. This leak filled the crawlspace of their home with gas, so when the furnace ignited that evening the explosion was disastrous.

The news was devastating to Velma, but we were in the perfect place to receive such disturbing news. The Broken Heart Club wept with us. At the same time, Velma's father George was struggling with dementia. A few months later, we lost our middle child by miscarriage. Then George went to heaven and six more of our immediate family also passed away. We lost 10 family members within the first 18 months of service to MFM. Given the fact that we had left excellent salaries behind and were living on a missionary allowance, many of our friends and neighbors thought we had lost our minds over religion. But the Broken Heart Club and other friends around the world have prayed us through every difficulty and every challenge.

Several of the men from this prayer group served on the OMS Board of Trustees and the MFM Cabinet. Their influence in southeastern Illinois via a monthly MFM prayer breakfast, a monthly prayer meeting, quarterly dinner meetings, annual picnics, annual banquets, and retreats resulted in some of us and our children becoming missionaries.

Max Edwards, missionary to Brazil, spoke at the closing session for the first retreat after I became a regional director. His challenge to obedience to God resulted in eight people repenting of their sins and inviting Jesus to be their Savior. One of the men who accepted Christ that evening was Paul Jones. Paul had been given an *ACTION* magazine, the magazine of Men for Missions, and was told he should go to one of the retreats listed in the magazine. Paul noticed our retreat in Albion, Illinois, and decided to drive the two and a half hours to attend the 7:00 a.m. breakfast to learn about these opportunities.

Paul was warm-hearted, intelligent, and open to a challenge. After he accepted Christ that evening, he volunteered to go to Brazil, South America, on a work team. At the close of the evening, people began to give him money for the Brazil work team. Late that night Paul drove home and the next morning he was at his church telling the congregation about his experience with the Lord and Max the day before, as well as his commitment to go to Brazil.

Paul was also kind and soft spoken. Growing up, he had always been told he was a "good boy." What did Paul do with his "good boy" image? He went to college and then to seminary and became a preacher, but he didn't have peace in his heart until that night in Albion with the Broken Heart Club when Howard Young prayed with him after Max Edwards' challenge.

All of us at the retreat instantly liked Paul. He began to travel with Howard and me, as well as with others. One of those trips was to North Dakota where he met several MFMers and shared about his trip to Brazil. Among the men in that crowd was Bud McWethy; Paul and Bud soon became good friends. Paul's continued involvement with MFM resulted in his wife Barbara and him becoming missionaries with OMS. You can read the rest of Paul Jones' story in *Still Sharpening.*

Over the years we hosted a multitude of missionaries at our meetings, which helped them get into churches throughout southern Illinois. This resulted in over 150 families going all over the world on MFM ministry teams. Millions of dollars have been given to OMS supporting the propagation of the Gospel. After spending hours on our knees, our prayers took legs and several of the members went to other states as well as out of the country. Those prayers carried me all over the central 14 states and then to 92 countries. Prayer is always the path to miracles, and I count it a blessing to have personally witnessed many of them.

Velma and I together have seen countless miracles of God because we have been privileged to live and work around men who saw themselves as common, yet took on jobs that needed to be done and, by God's grace and strength, they did them.

The Broken Heart Club attracted not only great missionaries from different nations but also administrators from headquarters in Greenwood, Indiana, who came to pray and be encouraged by the prayers of people who really cared about them.

Howard Young, then National Director of Men for Missions, spent extra time with us in our home. He traveled with me many times to Iowa, North Dakota, and most of my region. I watched my boss Howard draw stories out of men as he helped them recall what God did through them. It was miraculous. Many of these men didn't even realize they had been part of a miracle at the time it happened. After experiencing this revelation by talking with Howard, many men and their families were encouraged to take another step of faith to further enable the Gospel to go forward.

Like me, these men were common. Their faithfulness, however, resulted in continued generations who saw a need and helped. We have been privileged to associate with many of them and, in some cases, to learn that they are third- or even fourth-generation MFM participants. As Velma and I prepared to forward this chapter to our editing team today, we received the following note and a gift from a couple of third-generation members of the Broken Heart Club:

Hi, Warren and Velma,
I hope things are going well for you both. We pray for you every day.
We are busy planting beans. Corn is finished. God is good!
Love to both of you.
-Karl and Kathy

While we all see ourselves as common men, the glue that has kept us together has been the uncommon call to holiness expressed in the simple language asking if we will *Do whatever God asks us to do, Go wherever God asks, and Give whatever God asks.* We have found the Lord faithful as He has taken us all over the world to further His kingdom on earth. God has allowed me to give my testimony in more than 46 countries.

After hearing the testimony of Gideon Schlecht share about how God led him to Brazil, Otto "Bud" McWethy from North Dakota traveled to Colombia, South America, several times. He was a bold witness for Christ, a great friend, Bible scholar, and served for a time on staff with Evangelist Luis Palau. Bud allowed me to put his testimony in both *Iron Sharpens Iron* and *Still Sharpening*.

Another friend and colleague, Ed Fiorenza, translated *Iron Sharpens Iron* into Spanish, which made it available in several Spanish-speaking countries. On a trip to Cuba, a wonderful sister in the Lord asked to have her picture taken with me because *Iron Sharpens Iron* had encouraged her. This is the power of a testimony, just sharing truth with others.

"And they overcame him because of the blood of the Lamb and because of the word of their testimony, and they did not love their life even when faced with death" (Revelation 12:11).

The prayers of the Broken Heart Club are still being answered even today. I owe the Broken Heart Club and Jesus a debt I can never repay.

Where are the Great Men?

Warren Hardig

Where are the great men? "A righteous man who walks in his integrity – how blessed are his sons after him" (Proverbs 20:7).

Most of the time great men are where you least expect them to be, and they don't look like you think they should. It does not matter their country of origin or their language. The message from their hearts is more important than their grammar or their accent.

"As in water face reflects face, so the heart of man reflects man" (Proverbs 27:19).

A *real* man! What determines real manhood? Is it physical strength, possessions, or could it be something that many seek, yet never seem to grasp? Adding up capital assets is a poor way to measure the value of a man, because bank balances show nothing about how the capital was accumulated.

What does it take to be a real man? What do great men of God do? They do the little things that no one sees. My brother Bob and I, as well as my wife Velma, have something in common. We knew that our fathers would not tell a lie. We were taught by example that our word was our bond. Our fathers, Woodrow and George, were farmers, which of course means all three of us were farm kids. Our dads were always involved in helping neighbors at harvest time. Bob and I lost our dad at a young age when a blood clot struck his heart as he was helping to dig a neighbor's grave. How like him to die in service to someone! In those days when someone passed away it was normal for neighbors to take food to the family, dig the grave, and help harvest the crop if it was time. Velma's parents were more mobile than mine – and because of that, I have often said that George and Emma were the first missionaries I met.

One couple they ministered to lived in the country, about eight miles from town, who had many medical issues and didn't get around much. George and Emma took them groceries, medicine, and anything they needed, and spent time with them just being friends. One day while these friends were gone from their house, it caught fire and burned to the ground. Neighbors of those folks contacted George and Emma and gave them the news of their friends' loss. George and Emma positioned themselves at an intersection in town where their friends could be intercepted and have the bad news of their loss broken to them as gently as possible.

Our dads, Woodrow and George, were real men even though their names will never appear in print outside of this book. They lived simple lives in love and service to others.

Men like our fathers – real men, great men – are fortified by reading God's word. "With all prayer and petition pray at all times in the Spirit, and with this in view, be on the alert with all perseverance and petition for all the saints" (Ephesians 6:18). Most real men pray daily, "*Lord what do you have for me today?*" They take time to pray; they show kindness by listening and responding. Great men know you cannot be kind in a hurry.

A real man has a set of values that sustains him through life. Integrity, sexual purity, and honesty bring respect and trust to a man. The test of a real man is found in his integrity and character. "He who walks in integrity walks securely …" (Proverbs 10:9). I have always wanted to emulate the example they were to me.

During the peak season of the farm chemical business, some products radically varied in pricing, and some customers would spread rumors to drive the prices down. The company that was my major competitor had a Christian sales manager, Jack Brown. He and I always told the truth about our pricing. As a young businessman and a new Christian, I was fortunate to lean on the truth of Scripture: "How can a young man keep his way pure? By keeping it (his way) according to Your word. Your word I have treasured in my heart, that I may not sin against You" (Psalm 119:9, 11).

I sought to be marinated in God's Word. This isn't to say that I had all the answers; however, I walked in the light of the Word as truth was revealed to me. Being involved in Men for Missions has been my greatest blessing since becoming a Christian. It truly has been my life-changing adventure, for which I will be forever grateful.

A real man's senses are not dulled, nor is he blind to the needs around him. In fact, it is just the opposite, because caring for the needs of others becomes a priority. Wealth or poverty is not the common denominator – it is compassion. The men in Men for Missions have a global vision: they take steps forward in full surrender to *Do whatever God asks, Go wherever God asks, and Give whatever God asks.*

Tommy VanAbeele, a retired executive who has helped build ten homes for earthquake victims in Haiti, says, "Every time we finish a home, which will also be a ministry center, we pray with the new owners and hand them the keys. Then we cry." The only thing that can momentarily cloud a global vision is tears as we realize common men can be on the front lines for God.

God has put something in a man that will make him respond to the challenge of another man. "Iron sharpens iron, so one man sharpens another" (Proverbs 27:17). A real man has moral character that gives strength when the going gets tough. A real man overcomes the temptation to lie, to cut a corner, or to cheat on his wife. That strength comes from an intimate walk with God, who is perfect in His moral character.

I have mentioned that I came into Men for Missions through the Broken Heart Club. I remember those men and women who prayed over missionary prayer letters; they wept tears of love and compassion, and sought the Lord on behalf of those serving Him. He heard their prayers and provided. Everyone there was deeply invested in missions, and they consistently put their prayers into action. Their deep love was for those in missions and for those they wanted to reach. I had never seen people whose hearts were broken for the lost, and their hearts made a deep impression on mine.

The Strategic Importance of Men for Missions

Dr. David E. Dick

The first time I was introduced to MFM was when our best friends, who were accepted to serve with OMS, waited on a dark and dismally wet Friday night for a huge box truck to arrive at their home way out in the countryside of western Pennsylvania.

The truck arrived late in the evening, driven by a volunteer and accompanied by a rider/navigator, who gave their weekend to this unpaid labor of love to drive across three states to load and haul the personal possessions of our dear friends back to the Indiana headquarters of this mission organization.

I was touched by the self-sacrifice of these two men we had never met. They willingly worked long hours well into the night, packing and loading then jumping back into the truck, immediately leaving for the all-night return trip to Indianapolis.

Six years later when my wife Celia and I were accepted as members of this mission organization and were serving in the South Pacific, I got a full view of that same scene from the other side of the equation. I learned that MFM was composed almost entirely of laymen who volunteered their time for all kinds of mission activity, not just in their home countries but all around the world. These men sacrificially paid for their own travel; they used work vacations, family holidays, and personal time to assist in ministry outreach on the fields of OMS, both domestically and internationally.

I learned that to become a member of MFM, one had to commit to three things: willingness to *Do, Go, and Give* anything God asks of you. Simple, yet profound … and not altogether as easy as it sounds. Counting the cost can result in life-changing experiences where one's worldview is dramatically altered and one's heart is eternally transformed.

We were so far from headquarters, serving overseas in the South Pacific halfway around the world, that the only visitors we generally received were from the relatively nearby nation of Australia. Yet here again came the MFM folks who gave themselves away for the cause of Christ in a Muslim-majority nation. I was given great insight into what short-term missionaries could contribute to the overall goals of the mission. Resident missionaries would often have to wait months in order to gain an audience with a government official. Yet those same normally hard-nosed officials opened their office doors with a warm welcome and opened their hearts to the life-transforming testimonies of these honored guests who shared openly, freely, and effectively.

In later years, I saw this same level of lay effectiveness multiplied many times while serving as an officer of the mission and seeing the timely response from many laity who volunteered over and over again to assist practically, professionally, and personally with many diverse and demanding projects of OMS worldwide.

When a layperson goes cross cultural on his own nickel and stands before the local population to extend a winsome witness for Christ, people of all nationalities stand at attention (on the inside) and listen. God bless the men and women who have contributed to the cause of Christ around the world in support of OMS with MFM.

A Prisoner of Hope

Warren Hardig

I have had the privilege to work with and for wonderful people. When I worked in fertilizer sales, my financial success depended upon what I was able to sell and deliver in April, May, and June, since those are the months farmers apply their fertilizer. Sure, there was product to be delivered in September and October; however, the second quarter of the year was my time to make a living.

To withstand all the pressure, I had to guard what was important: peace in my heart and mind. Protecting my heart literally meant a continued deliverance from the habit of smoking that was killing me.

Delivering product invariably involved 18-hour days. The steering wheel and the cab of an International truck was the altar where I constantly prayed. The verse that played on my mind was, "I love those who love Me; and those who diligently seek Me will find Me" (Proverbs 8:17). My faith strengthened as God answered prayers, helping me deliver product to the plant, keeping the equipment from breaking down, handling customer complaints, and selling. Six months after my resignation and new career with MFM, I received my largest bonus check from the work I had done that spring.

In the nearly five years between my salvation and joining the staff at MFM, Velma and I had become youth leaders at our little Methodist church after one of the church ladies prayed us into the position. We started out with three young ladies attending, and it soon increased, growing to nearly 40 young folks. It was exciting to see a new young person came to faith in Christ nearly every week. We met every Sunday night and always closed our meetings with prayers together at the altar of the church unless we were at our home for a party or the nearby lake and cabin for a weekend retreat.

Our dream home, set on two acres with lots of trees and flowers, was ideal for the kids. And not just the kids. When I turned into the driveway after work, I was happy to be home. It was not unusual to see kids scattered all over the property. They loved us, and we loved them.

At church, there would be times we would be reading devotions and someone would grab the person next to them and take them to the altar to pray. Most of our free time, if it wasn't with the youth, was spent with our preacher and his family. These people became our biggest sacrifice to leave behind for our next steps in MFM and OMS.

With two small children, the pastor and his wife found it hard to arrange an extended vacation. We had a new car and no children at the time, so the six of us drove out to the Grand Tetons and Yellowstone Park for a week or so to give them a break. The rest of the time Velma and I were at home and were frequently doing something for the church, or I might have been shooting trap at one of the gun clubs. I have always loved hunting and shooting sports.

The preacher worked with me intensely for more than a year to help me grow spiritually – it felt like he had to start from below zero! I had no idea who God was or what His character was like, and I was totally ignorant of what was in the Bible. Most days we talked about his sermon and what we were reading. We also prayed together every evening, at the altar, before we locked the church for the night.

Now several years and three or four million miles over the U.S. and 90 countries later, I claim another verse of Scripture as my own: "May it never be that I would boast, except in the cross of our Lord Jesus Christ, through which the world has been crucified to me, and I to the world" (Galatians 6:14).

Testimonies of Christ's forgiveness and guidance will transcend any cultural, racial, or linguistic barrier. That is what this book is about. These global testimonies speak for themselves. The power of a testimony: "And they overcame him because of the blood of the Lamb and because of the word of their testimony, and they did not love their life even when faced with death" (Revelation 12:11).

Evangelist Luis Palau said it well: "One encounter with Jesus Christ is enough to change you, instantly, forever."

One time while in India, I was asked to speak to a large group of people. I remember sitting on the platform thinking, *What have I got to say to these people?* So, I did what I always do: I gave my testimony, then presented an invitation to accept Christ.

That altar was packed. I remember a blind man who asked me to pray for his sight to be restored. There was also a young girl in a red sari who was praying for a job. She was very young, but so many people were depending on her for food. I think seven or eight people asked Jesus into their hearts. None of this was my doing. I felt totally inadequate. It was because of Jesus and His finished work on the cross. My prayer and testimony are Psalm 115:1: "Not to us, oh Lord, not to us, but to Your name give glory because of Your lovingkindness, because of Your truth."

I must acknowledge the Broken Heart Club and my faithful prayer partners and supporters, both before and after we had children. My friend and brother John McLaughlin has traveled with me to more than 30 countries. We still endeavor to pray together every day, even though we live several hundred miles apart.

In recent years, Velma has been able to travel with me regularly, yet nothing has happened in my life without her blessing and prayer support. She was trustworthy to represent me in meetings when I was away, which was most of the time. She was home caring for Roger and Reneé and keeping our home intact. Velma is and was my anchor, keeping things stable, standing by me (if not physically, always in prayer), and encouraging me in prayer to be obedient, knowing that obedience is better than sacrifice. "Samuel said, 'Has the Lord as much delight in burnt offerings and sacrifices as in obeying the voice of the Lord? Behold, to obey is better than sacrifice, and to heed than the fat of rams'" (1 Samuel 15:22).

I am a prisoner of hope.

No Dunk Tank for Me

Doug Tankersley

Introduction by Warren Hardig

Doug Tankersley, like all the men in this book who have shared part of their pilgrimage with us, has a keen mind and a heart to serve God. Doug and Cindy are a team who complement each other wherever they are serving. Doug capably relates to the Latin American culture and strongly encourages our brothers and sisters in Cuba, Ecuador, and Colombia.

Doug is a great boots-on-the-ground man for our MFM ministry teams serving OMS-related churches in Colombia. He is a capable and a detail-oriented person, giving our teams comfortable, clean accommodations with wholesome food, keeping us all healthy. Doug always has literature – Bibles for our use, and Spanish Bibles for us to give those who pray to receive Christ.

Being bilingual gives him the advantage of understanding more clearly the culture and what is going on around him. No matter what language Doug is speaking, it is full of love and concern for the eternal destiny of their souls. Here is his story, in his own words …

Growing up in a small central Illinois farm community, I had no idea what a missionary was. In fact, I had never even heard of one. I attended church occasionally with my mom and sisters when it was convenient. Other than a couple of songs, I don't even remember hearing much about Jesus during that time. After completing high school, I moved away and began attending Eastern Illinois University with plans to eventually teach industrial arts, although I nearly flunked out my first year due to my lack of dedication to my bookwork and taking school seriously.

When I was 21 years old, I met Cindy, who would become my best friend and the love of my life, on a blind date. She helped me get my act together and I completed a graduate program while somehow making it onto the Dean's list. I'm still not sure how that happened!

We were married two years later and in 1987 moved to Florida, where Cindy taught first grade and I taught junior high industrial arts, but only for six weeks. I quickly recognized that teaching junior high kids was not for me and discovered I could make a lot more money as an engineer for a power boat company in Orlando. So I took that job, and a year and a half later was asked to manage the engineering and quality assurance department at their newest plant. So, we packed up and headed to Tennessee.

While living in Tennessee, we had good jobs, nice vehicles, a new boat, and a new house. I felt like we had it all. I even foolishly put a bumper sticker on our boat trailer that read: "In the end, the one with the most toys wins."

Yet I felt like something was still missing from my life, though I didn't know what it was. One day Cindy told me she would like to begin attending church and she would like me to go with her. I thought, *Sure, I used to go to church off and on when I was a kid. Why not?*

The Baptist church we began attending was just completing a week of Vacation Bible School, and they were having baptisms for the youth who had recently made decisions to accept Jesus as their

Savior. I had never seen baptisms by immersion and had no idea what was taking place. I remember leaning over and smugly telling Cindy, "They ain't never getting me in that dunk tank."

Shortly after that, the church had a revival with a guest preacher who asked all of us attending, "If you walk out that door tonight and are hit by a car and die, would you be in heaven or in hell?" Wow, that question really caught my attention! I had no idea whether I would be in heaven or hell, and I didn't know if anyone could actually know for sure. I felt I was better than a lot of other people and there were others a lot worse than me, but was that good enough?

Then the preacher said, "If you walk out that door and die tonight, and you know without a doubt that if you die you will be in heaven, I want you to raise your hand." I looked around and saw most of the hands up in the air. I thought, *How is that possible? How can they be so sure? I want to have that confidence - but how?* I wanted to know how I could be with Jesus in heaven if I died.

About that same time, Cindy took a week to visit family in Illinois while I stayed home for work. During that time, a three-night miniseries called "Jesus of Nazareth" was broadcast on network TV. I began to watch that show, and each night I was amazed at what I was listening to. During commercial breaks I would look in the Bible at what I had just heard; I was amazed that what they were saying was exactly the same in the Bible.

As I look back upon that time, I have no idea how I could have found those related passages in the Bible I did not know. It had to have been through divine intervention. Because of that show, I discovered I was a sinner in need of a Savior and having a personal relationship with Jesus was missing in my life. So I prayed and asked Jesus into my heart and accepted Jesus as my Lord and Savior.

Since that time my life has never been the same. I had no idea how Jesus would so radically change my life in 1990. I discovered I could have an incredible personal and genuine relationship with my Heavenly Father and He wanted an intimate relationship with me. I also gained 100 percent assurance that if I die today, I will be in heaven. I could now confidently raise my hand if asked by that pastor.

I was also quite surprised that after I had made the most important decision of my life, Cindy confided in me and confessed that she had recruited other believers who, with her, had been praying for me and for my salvation. I can't begin to describe the joy, excitement, and hope I now felt as a child of God. I could not wait to be baptized in that "dunk tank" as a profession of my faith in Jesus. Cindy was also baptized as she rededicated her life in Christ. We were blessed to attend a church that preached and actually taught the Word of God directly from the Bible. Like a sponge, I absorbed all I could.

When I began working for that powerboat company, I had no idea they were a Christian-owned company, nor would I have really cared. But they weren't afraid to be quite open about their beliefs, and I soon began to receive invitations from fellow employees to go on a short-term mission trips. I admit I had no idea what they were talking about or why I would want to go.

I remember first being exposed to short-term missions as I watched a video of those who had just returned from their trips. I was intrigued, and began to understand how Jesus was calling us to be His disciples and to *Go*. I continued to receive many invitations over the years, and had all the excuses why I shouldn't go: I had small children, no time off of work, too expensive, too dangerous, can't leave my family, etc. I had also previously convinced myself that if I ever did go on a short-term mission trip, I wanted it to be on a work team where I could use my hands and not have to share my testimony or the Gospel, thinking I might mess that up and just confuse people. What I didn't take into account was that the Lord could use me beyond my abilities if I would allow Him.

In 1996 we moved to Illinois where we began attending Gibson City Bible Church, which had a heart for supporting missions. Each year they held an annual missions conference where they invited some of the missionaries they supported to share with the church. It was through these missions conferences we became acquainted with Kent Eller, then National Director for Men for Missions. Cindy and I, along with our two boys, were attracted to Kent's winning personality and his passion for missions. Kent stayed in our home while attending the annual conference, and our two boys loved hearing Kent's tales from across the world. We spent the evenings asking Kent questions and listening to stories of how God was using ordinary laymen and their families to accomplish incredible things. Our interest in missions and serving continued to grow.

In 2000, I received another invitation to go on a short-term mission trip from Tim K., the vice president of the Christian boat company whose workers never gave up on inviting me. Tim warned me this particular trip would be the most physically and spiritually challenging of my life, and I would return home radically changed. He told me we would be hiking into five remote villages in the jungles of Guatemala to evangelize in unreached areas. It was not a work team! At that time I was attending a weekly men's Bible study on the book of James, and during that study, James 1:22 seemed to embolden me. The words lifted off the page: "Do not merely listen to the Word, and so deceive yourselves. Do what it says." As I read those words, I remembered Jesus tells us to "Go therefore and make disciples of all the nations" (Matthew 28:19), so how could I say "No"? I knew with complete confidence God was calling me to *Go*.

I said "Yes," and joined the all-men team. My first short-term mission trip involved 11 different airplanes and one bus. The smaller single-engine Cessnas had no seats and were covered with duct tape, and the landing strips were simple cattle trails in the clearings. There were no roads to the remote villages so we hiked, carrying everything from village to village. In the first remote jungle village, I vividly remember the missionary asking our team members that evening who would be the first to share their testimony and getting a response of complete silence, which lasted long enough for me to process in my mind that I had not come all this way to be silent. I had a story to tell, so I volunteered to share.

Our team had carried in a generator, flood lamp, portable microphone and speaker. In complete darkness, one team member held the flood light in my face as I nervously shared my testimony how Jesus had transformed my life, while attempting to keep moths and other bugs attracted to the light from flying into my mouth. It took me traveling over a thousand miles to share my personal testimony for the first time!

Tim was right. It was the most physically and spiritually challenging trip I have ever been on. It was extremely hot and humid, and we were continually attacked by biting bugs. The hikes between villages were strenuous as we carried everything we needed. Some villages welcomed our arrival, others did not. Sleeping arrangements ranged from animal shelters filled with cockroaches to nights on the ground under the stars when a village would not provide us shelter. We pressed on, fueled by potatoes, which eventually ran out, and purified water from mud puddles when our water also ran out. I discovered what it was like to live by faith alone and watch the Lord provide.

On that trip, I also had the opportunity to see a glimpse of Jesus in action as I witnessed the on-field missionary and national pastors exhibit their authentic compassion to see lost souls getting saved. I had never seen anything like that and found it amazing to behold.

During one of my personal morning devotion times, I vividly remember watching a young child laughing and having the time of his life as he played with the remnant of a popped balloon (from those we had handed out the day before), when I felt the Lord asking me to surrender my agenda for His agenda. We continued that week showing the "Jesus" movie where we could, performing dramas for the children and sharing the Gospel to all who would listen.

Again Tim was right. I returned home radically changed, knowing I was being called to full-time service for the Lord, though having no idea what that meant. During the next couple years, I prayed for the Lord's leading, focused on building our local church's short-term mission program, and led a team to Guatemala. I came back on fire for the Lord. I could not help but think, *If the Lord can use my gifts and talents overseas, why can't He use them here at home?* These short-term trips provided me with boldness to share my testimony and the Gospel with my coworkers and even my mom, who prayed to receive Christ while sitting at our kitchen table.

In 2002, my missionary friends John and Rita shared with me about an 18-year-old El Salvadorian man named Duglas who had felt God's call to serve as the pastor in Ingenio, a remote little village in Guatemala. The adobe dirt floor church where he was serving was very small and in poor condition, with a congregation of only six women. Duglas could not afford a house, so he had partitioned off a

5' x 5' area in the corner of the church with sheets of tin and boards for his bedroom. He had no kitchen or bathroom and relied solely on the Lord to provide.

John and Rita shared with me their desire to build a house for this young pastor on the land next to the church. I immediately felt the Lord's leading to help dear, faithful Duglas, so I quickly received approval from our church leadership to raise interest and funds. We had plans to send a group of men and their wives to help with construction. Since there were only women in the Ingenio church, we thought it best to have our wives with us. (Notice I said "we" thought our wives should go along with us).

As we generated interest in having couples on the trip, several of us experienced complications with children and home responsibilities and realized the difficulties the trip would place on our wives. We also became aware that in Ingenio, our team would need to stay and sleep on the dirt floor inside the tiny one-room church. It would be difficult to have men and women in the same room with no privacy for dressing and changing clothes, and there was not enough floor space for everyone to sleep. Bathrooms, running water, hotels, and housing did not exist. Could it be the Lord desired our team to be men only?

In 2003, I had the opportunity to organize and lead a team of nine men from our church to go to Ingenio to help with the construction of Duglas's house. This was the first time for the majority of these men to be outside the U.S., visiting and working in a poor village in a foreign country like Guatemala. It was a real stretch for all of us as we ate black beans three times a day, showered in the rain, and used a makeshift latrine that often flooded.

The church sat next to the main dirt road through town and was in a good location for all who passed by to stop and observe a group of white gringos working hard. Despite working hard from sunrise to sunset, we were having a good time, laughing and enjoying our time with each other, as well as with Pastor Duglas, the construction maestro (foreman), and the ladies from the church. We always had a crowd of people watching whenever we were working, mostly men from the village.

The six ladies from the church were all married, but their husbands were not attending church because they believed attending church was only for women; it was no place for tough men. Ingenio was strongly Roman Catholic, and to attend this Protestant church would be inviting social and political problems into their lives. Evangelical Christians were not even welcome in this village. We worked hard and completed the house in a week and had a great time while ministering to our sisters in Christ, their children, Pastor Duglas, and several schools in the area. It was truly a life-changing journey for every team member. We returned home, sore but very blessed.

In 2004, we were attending another annual Missions Conference where Kent Eller was one of the main speakers. I remember Cindy becoming a bit restless, and her tears began to flow. Through the words being spoken that weekend, she knew the Lord was calling her to surrender all to Him and calling us to full-time mission service. We had no idea what to do with this and didn't know if any mission would accept us, since we were in our 40s and were working in secular jobs, but Kent suggested we consider applying to One Mission Society. We began the application and interview process, and were ecstatic when OMS accepted us.

Since we felt the Lord leading us to full-time mission work with OMS, we wanted to get away and seek the Lord's direction in our lives, especially our future country of service. I returned to Ingenio later in

2004 and took Cindy with me, so we could spend some quiet time with the Lord. We had the pleasure of visiting with Pastor Duglas, who was now taking seminary classes through rural extension courses. We even had the incredible opportunity to sleep in the house we men had built.

One evening as we were preparing to show movies on a makeshift screen between the church and the house, I was amazed to see a group of men scurrying around, arranging the church benches and preparing things for the event. I wondered aloud who these men were, and Pastor Duglas explained they were 16 new members of the church who had taken on leadership positions. I asked Pastor Duglas what had taken place since our team had been there, and he explained that our all-man team had been a huge influence on these local men. The men admitted they attended the church now because of our team's actions for Christ and how we had treated the men and their wives while we were there.

Pastor Duglas also explained the men were attending church now because they could see us Christian gringos having a great time, working very hard from sunrise to sunset, even though our wives were not with us. It was clear to them our team was there because we wanted to serve the Lord and not because our wives insisted. They realized the church was not just for women, and they wanted to see what the gringos had in their lives that they did not have.

Our influence as Christians is powerful, and it seems to happen when we are not even aware of it. As always, God had a plan. Our team planned to have our wives go with us, but the Lord knew the men of Ingenio needed to see the Christian gringos as part of the church without their wives. I had the pleasure to speak with Pastor Duglas five years later, and they had 80 adults and 80 children in this church. Our home church eventually raised funds to help them build a new, larger church. What a testimony! How the Lord used our simple acts of obedience, and used the influence of our all-man team, to change the men in that village!

By 2005, we were raising support as career missionaries to Ecuador. We had become the talk of our small hometown as people wondered why in the world we would give up everything and move our family overseas. In 2006, we excitedly left our secure secular jobs, sold everything we owned, and moved our family to live and serve the Lord full time in Ecuador.

I had the privilege of serving as a liaison between OMS and the Association of Evangelical Churches of Ecuador, working with 12 national churches in the central district. I saw much of the country of Ecuador and got to know and serve with many pastors and church members who had been persecuted for their faith in Christ. What an honor to serve with those folks and what an influence they were in strengthening my walk and boldness in the Lord. We also had opportunities to host several MFM work and evangelism teams, and our familiarity and relationship with MFM continued to grow.

In 2010, when our four-year term in Ecuador was completed, we were required by the mission to return to Illinois for furlough, a time to share with supporting churches and individuals about our past four years while raising financial support to return. However, shortly after we had returned, my dad passed away, leaving Mom home alone with no other family close by. Also, our younger son had a difficult time adjusting to living in a foreign city of 2.5 million people, so we explored the idea of remaining in Illinois for four years until he completed high school. It was especially difficult for me not to return to Ecuador as planned, for I had made many good friends and relationships. I also felt I had not completed the work in which I had been involved. We were at a loss what to do.

We contacted Kent Eller at MFM to see if they needed a regional director in Illinois and were so glad to find out they did. We soon began training, leading, and taking MFM short-term teams to the field. In November 2011, Greg Carlson (then serving as the OMS Every Community for Christ church multiplication facilitator for Colombia and Ecuador) and I had the opportunity to join a team of 56 North Americans and an estimated 150 to 175 Colombians. We partnered to share the Gospel of Jesus Christ by going door to door in the coastal city of Barranquilla, Colombia. It was a fruitful time of evangelizing and discipling new believers. The fields in this area were ripe spiritually, and the people were so open and hungry to hear about the saving grace of Jesus Christ.

We joined a team led by the mission e3 Partners, which provided a wonderful opportunity for Greg and me to learn more about their mission organization as we jointly worked towards saturating Colombia with the Gospel. During that week, 1,578 people prayed to receive Christ and hundreds more heard the Gospel. I wondered how or why there were so many decisions for Christ in one week and discovered that Colombia had been and continues to be bathed in prayer, led by OMS, that their hearts would be softened and open to receive Christ.

I knocked on many doors in Barranquilla with my translator and shared my personal testimony concerning the way Jesus had changed my life. I was never rejected from a visit. I shared the Gospel by using the EvangeCube™* *(as shown)* and offered those listening the opportunity to make a personal decision of faith and to accept Jesus as their Lord and Savior. Some responded by telling me how hope and trust in Jesus was exactly what they had been searching for. Others immediately wanted me to share with their family members so they, too, could have eternal hope and be saved. It was such an amazing experience to see someone at the door allow me to share with them and watch the scowl on their face change to a smile with tears as they accepted Jesus as their Savior. I saw the Lord touch the hearts of 16 people that week as they responded to Him with professions of faith while many more listened.

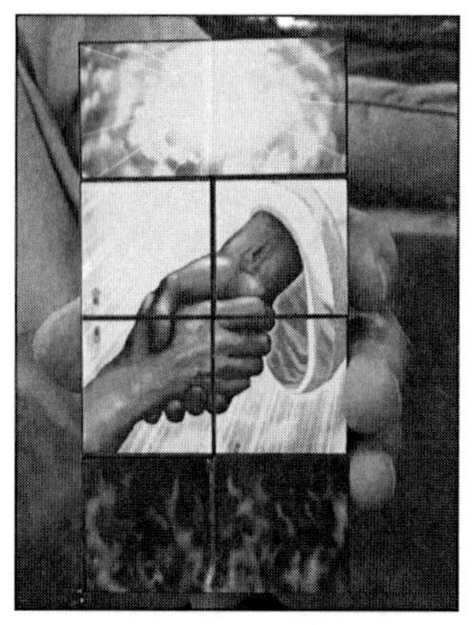

I was awed that the Lord could use me in such a simple and fun way of sharing Jesus with those waiting to hear about Him. Romans 10:17 reminds us that faith comes from hearing the message, and the message is heard through the Word of Christ. Isaiah 55:11 tells us that the Word of God will not return void. This team definitely planted seeds!

In 2012, MFM began leading evangelism teams to Colombia to serve alongside Project Satura and to support project "Saturation Antioquia," which included the goal of planting 20,000 house churches in five years within the department (region) of Antioquia, Colombia. As we attempted to raise teams for the trip, we found it difficult to find people willing to go. Just mentioning the name Colombia, what with its past reputation, scared people away. They were also intimidated by the idea of door-to-door evangelism. OMS did not have any on-field missionaries to receive and host the teams there. We were only able to raise one team in 2012 and three in 2013. It was difficult to find folks willing to take the step of faith.

As I led teams, I could see that the fields of Colombia were ripe for harvest and that we needed more teams to come alongside our national partners. In the spring of 2013, I contacted OMS's Human Resources Department and asked about the possibility of having missionaries there receive teams. I knew OMS had not sent any missionaries to that country for about 15 years and we wouldn't likely be considered since we were planning to return to Ecuador in 2014. As I continued to lead teams in Columbia, I could feel the Lord impressing upon my heart the need to surrender our plans of returning to Ecuador and prayerfully consider serving in Colombia to help host MFM evangelism teams. Doing so would reduce the workload for our Satura ministry partners currently fulfilling that responsibility, and could also help provide a sense of security for MFM short termers by knowing OMS had missionaries living on the field.

During our time in Ecuador, we never had the opportunity to invest much time learning the Spanish language. As we prepared to return, we decided to spend nine months in Costa Rica attending language school. I still felt the burden of needing missionaries in Colombia to help receive the MFM teams, so we asked Kent about the possibility of serving as missionaries with MFM in Colombia to help receive teams and train the nationals to do so as well. He didn't think that was possible, but said he would check into it.

In July 2014, we began attending language classes and were preparing to return to Ecuador, but were longing to move to Colombia to help with the evangelism efforts. Meanwhile, Kent was busy working on the possibilities of us serving on behalf of MFM in Colombia.

In December 2014, we received word that it might be possible to serve in Colombia, serving directly with Igleico, the national church denomination started by OMS years before. We were to fly to Colombia for a week of interviews to see if we would be a good fit to help them and also interview them about their plans and vision. In January 2015, we were thrilled the President of Igleico invited us to come and serve with them, focusing on hosting MFM evangelism teams supporting Satura, training other Colombians to host teams, and sharing an awareness of MFM in Colombia. We were empowered to challenge Colombian laymen and their families to *Do, Go and Give* in total obedience to Jesus Christ. In July 2015, we moved to Medellín, Colombia. With our presence on the field, along with reports coming back from team members, we began to see an increase in the size and number of our evangelism teams. We soon had no problem filling teams and even had a waiting list for future teams.

By November 2017, Cindy and I recognized we had completed what we went to Colombia to do. We had hosted and led many MFM evangelism teams, trained 13 Satura facilitators to receive teams, and introduced MFM to about 100 Colombian churches. Jonathan T. served as our first MFM Facilitator, taking over hosting teams when they arrived. We were no longer needed in Colombia; it was time to allow them to assume the responsibility and grow their ministry. So we moved back to the States.

As missionaries currently serving in the U.S., we have many opportunities to visit churches, share with groups, and speak with individuals about the openings to serve on short-term missions trips through MFM. We do so with enthusiastic hearts, knowing the amazing ways God can use MFM to be a life-changing journey.

On various occasions we have been asked why someone should serve overseas when we have needs here in the United States. Having worked on a farm years ago, I helped harvest corn and soybeans. It was always important to have the equipment prepared and ready and when the fields were ripe for harvest, it was crucial to gather the crops immediately. If you waited too long, much of the potential harvest would be lost. Timing was essential. The response to "Why serve overseas?" has never been clearer to me. It is important to serve and share the Gospel of Jesus Christ where the fields are ripe for harvest.

I have been serving in missions for only 15 years, but I have never seen the fields as ripe for harvest as they currently are in Colombia. In John 4:35, Jesus tells his disciples: "I tell you, open your eyes and look at the fields! They are ripe for harvest."

The fields are truly ripe. Between 2012 to 2020, there have been 40 MFM evangelism teams with 322 short-term team members who went to Colombia and over 15,000 people made decisions of faith. I continue to receive reports on how churches trained by our MFM teams are continuing to evangelize their own community and surrounding communities with the Gospel. They are also training others without us being there, and the number of decisions of faith continues to increase. And to think … years ago I decided that if I ever went on a short-term missions trip, I wanted to be on a work team, not an evangelism team.

I continually thank the Lord that when short-term missions trip opportunities were presented to me and although I used a plethora of excuses not to go, the Lord never gave up on me, nor did my friend Tim. This is a good reminder of the importance of continuing to invite first timers on short-term missions trips, and not giving up on any invited in the past.

We continue living in the U.S., and I am serving as Regional Director for Latin America. We focus on leading teams and introducing MFM to new Latin American countries, including the islands of Dominican Republic and Cuba. In 2019, we began leading evangelism teams, working with our Cuban church partners and, like Colombia, were seeing an incredible openness and thirst for the living water only Jesus can provide. Our all-men teams and the ministry of Men for Missions attracted the attention of the Cuban men, and today Allen Q. is our national MFM director in Cuba.

MFM-Cuba now has groups of MFM men located within various communities across the island and they are active, operating in a way that MFM did when it was first founded. They have been an inspiration to us as they have formed action groups that network across the island and work together as needed.

A house church in Cuba.

During the difficult days of COVID, they actively fed the hungry, provided beds and wheelchairs. They tracked down and provided critically needed medicines, always sharing the Gospel, providing toys to children, and helping those who lost homes to fires or tornadoes. The list goes on and on. This is an incredible team that glorifies God while challenging men to *Do, Go and Give* in total obedience to Jesus Christ.

I am thankful that some borders have opened and we can begin to travel freely with teams again. I am also passionate about the idea of seeing some of our future MFM teams consist of team members from various countries, international team members mixed together as one team working on projects and serving together side by side.

It's been a wild ride with the Lord since I accepted Jesus as my Savior, and I remain humbled that God could use someone like me, an ordinary man, in Ecuador, in Colombia, and now as a Regional Director with Men for Missions in Latin America. Short-term mission trips truly are a life-changing journey.

I finally said "Yes" to going on a short-term mission trip in 2001 and came home radically changed. I had no idea where that first trip would lead, and I have no regrets. I can't wait to see what the Lord has in store next. My prayer is, "You lead, Lord, and I'll follow."

Doug has been appointed Vice Executive Director of Men for Missions Global.

How Do You Define Success?

Warren Hardig

How do you define success? Before I met Jesus, I would say, "I have simple tastes – the *best* will always do."

Succeeding more in business, driving new vehicles, owning a beautiful home in the country, belonging to the right lodge, eating at the best restaurants, and enjoying the Rocky Mountains on vacation were all on my *To Do* list, with an emphasis on one thing: *more*. I was not unusual; that is how many Americans spell success.

My culture began to change when I knelt on a concrete floor at the farm chemical business I managed, and asked God to forgive my sins, starting with my vocabulary, then my value system. Now in the 21st Century, it seems our culture is changing the church, rather than the church changing the culture. This is because our message from the church, while biblically based, lacks the strong Gospel message about Jesus.

Could it be we are focused on mission statements and core values without a message of repentance and surrender to Jesus Christ? I have heard it said that churches are controlled by fear: fear they won't like us, fear our music won't be right, fear the people won't come, or fear that we won't be politically correct in this day of off-the-chart sensitivities.

One of the missing ingredients in today's church is compassion for others and concern about where they will spend eternity. I joined a Men for Missions ministry team to Haiti and received a crash course in compassion.

I often tell people that going on a ministry team with Men for Missions can be hazardous to your ambitions. My statement to you about your life-changing journey with Men for Missions is: "I don't want you to have a good trip. I want you to have a great trip – a trip so great that you say to your friends, 'The next time I go, you *have* to go with me.'"

Most of these short-term trips involve a lot of travel, which was much more enjoyable prior to 9/11. You were allowed to take more luggage, which was a blessing when traveling to multiple countries. I would often facilitate teams going to a minimum of four countries. It is no surprise that travelers who visited Korea, Japan, Hong Kong, China, and Taiwan would find many treasures along the way. I purchased a handmade porcelain lamp, a beautiful wool rug, and a few other small treasures. My teammates did likewise.

I had been told when I arrived in Taiwan, the last stop on a five-country tour, that we could leave our luggage and the objects we had purchased "in bond." Leaving your items "in bond" meant they would be safe and secure at the airport for the time we were in that country. However, one very important piece of information I didn't hear was that when placing luggage in bond, it was to be ticketed to your next port. In our case, the next port was home.

I had purchased a beautiful rug in China. Trying to be a good leader, I encouraged our folks to leave all the luggage we could in bond to help our hosts in Taiwan. I put my rug and four other pieces in bond.

Early on the morning of our departure I went to the airport, approached the ticket agent with confidence and presented my claim checks for the items in bond. The lady behind the counter didn't know what to do. She quickly turned to the agent at the next terminal, who was equally at a loss on what to do. They advised me that I had put them in bond, but I hadn't given any of the required forwarding information.

One of the ladies called her supervisor, getting the gentleman out of bed, and it wasn't long before the United Airlines supervisor appeared and escorted me to the basement of the Chiang Kai-shek Airport.

Do you have any idea how much luggage can be loaded into seven 747 airplanes? Imagine it! There was a sea of luggage before us, and every single one had a ticket on it.

The United supervisor called some employees over and handed them my luggage tickets. Off they went to retrieve my items, leaving the supervisor and me at the entrance of this vast basement with countless pieces of luggage to be loaded into the airplanes getting ready to depart that morning.

My new Chinese acquaintance spoke English well. I began an attempt to share Scripture, going down the Roman Road* and then to Titus 3:3-7. He told me he was a Buddhist, which should have put an end to the conversation. I could see in the distance the United employees had found my rug and were coming toward us. I boldly yet gently said, "I would like to recommend you consider Christianity. Before I became a Christian, I was afraid to die."

He looked at me and responded, "I am afraid to die."

The employees returned and the two of us took the treasures up the escalator. As we went up the escalator, I shared the Gospel with my new friend, telling him how the Lord had taken away my fear of dying when I surrendered my life to Him.

His work with me was finished, yet he stayed with me, quite literally, until I was at the cabin door to board the 747 for the trip across the Pacific. I'll never know this side of heaven if he accepted Christ into his heart, but there was no doubt he was impacted by the promise of life without fear of death.

What a relief it was to fasten my seat belt before takeoff. I found myself seated between a Chinese gentleman to my left and my Pentecostal preacher to my right. I struck up a conversation with the Chinese gentleman and, eventually, while flying high above the Pacific Ocean, he prayed to receive Christ as his Savior.

Not long after this life-changing encounter, I went back to the galley and asked the young Korean cabin attendant if I could have a Coke. It was a simple exchange, but as she began pouring my beverage into a cup, she asked without looking up at me, "How do you get your answers from God?"

I took the opportunity to quietly tell her how to get answers from God. Our interaction was brief but impactful.

When you witness for God, you never know who may be listening or watching. It is very important to pray over our actions and reactions as we go through life.

My beautiful rug, the one that caused me so much trouble, is in the hall in front of the bedroom door, but my most precious treasure is the Gospel of Jesus Christ.

How do I define success now? "He who is wise wins souls" (Proverbs 11:30, NASB 1995).

**For The Roman Road, See Appendix A*

Dwight Ferguson

Warren Hardig

Dwight Ferguson, founder of Men for Missions, said, "You don't join Men for Missions, you get right with God and Men for Missions will join you."

When Dwight asked God, "How do we reach the multitudes of Asia?" God gave him one word: *Laymen.* The fuel that propels Men for Missions forward is laymen with hearts filled with Christ's love for the world.

Dwight also said, "We take men to the mission field and bring them home full of compassion they didn't have when they left." When we return home with this new level of compassion, it is our privilege and responsibility to represent those who can't represent themselves.

Laymen and their families still reach across linguistic, cultural, and racial barriers with the goal of encouraging the lordship of Jesus Christ in each man's life at home and around the world.

Dwight's spirit lives on in many of us. I have many memories of the fiery Ferguson preaching in southern Illinois. If Dwight was preaching and we could make it to the venue, you could find Velma and me in the second or third row every night. The revivals usually ran seven days with morning Bible studies and evangelistic evenings with serious calls for unbelievers to repent and give their lives to Jesus.

On one occasion in Mt. Carmel, Illinois, the evangelism outreach was scheduled for one week in a small church. However, the attendance and movement of God's Spirit called for a second week in a larger church and then another bigger church, ending up after six weeks in a school gymnasium to hold an even larger crowd. Dwight prayed with people on the sidewalk and in restaurants. The music in the restaurants was even cleaned up due to Dwight's preaching on repentance. The whole community was changed.

The Gospel message Ferguson preached had a profound impact in several areas. A few years ago, while attending a Baptist church in Carmi, Illinois, with our friends Dean and Barbara Baker, Dean introduced me to an older gentleman and told him I was with Men for Missions. He asked, "Do you know Dwight Ferguson?"

I replied in the affirmative.

He then told me, "Dwight Ferguson led me to the Lord in a doghouse* while I was working in the oil field." He went on to say that when Dwight came on the scene around the drilling rig, the language of the workers immediately changed.

Dwight could talk to you about oil exploration, the population of the corn you were planting, or any subject, but somewhere in the conversation the matter of Jesus Christ, God's Son, would be brought in. Dwight set Men for Missions aflame when he said, "Dare we believe God will put His hand on a dozen, a hundred or a thousand men to obediently carry out the Great Commission? This could revolutionize modern missions." Thousands of men and women have believed God and trusted Him to bring His Word to life through their doing, going, and giving. To God be the glory!

"Go therefore and make disciples of all the nations, baptizing them in the name of the Father and the Sn and Holy Spirit" (Matthew 28:19).

Two Gold Rings

Warren Hardig

My first overseas experience with Men for Missions was in Haiti. I worked as a regional director approximately six years before I was assigned in 1979 to lead a trip to Asia that included Japan, South Korea, Hong Kong, and Taiwan. I was eager and excited about this assignment; however, I was also scared. Dwight Ferguson, the founder of MFM and his wife, Stella, were on the trip.

Our first stop was Japan, where we spoke in churches, met the missionaries, and learned more about the country where OMS began ministry in 1901. Dwight and Stella were distinguished servants and highly respected all over the world. Dwight was preaching in Asia some years before when their son Marvin was killed in a hunting accident in Colorado. We had other distinguished guests on the trip with us to help dedicate this new church in South Korea in honor of Marvin.

Then it was on to South Korea, where Dr. J.B. Crouse was our host and gave us a wonderful tour of the OMS work there. On one of the days, J.B. took us to visit a leper colony. When J.B. drove us through a construction site then walked us through a chicken house and hog barn, it was quite an experience for the city dwellers on our team. For me, having grown up on the farm, those were familiar sights and smells. Also, I had a bit of pride because Men for Missions had provided hogs and chickens, smell and all, for these rejects of society, as a means of livelihood for them.

We soon found out that Dwight and Stella had previously visited the same leper colony during the Korean War. Dwight had preached in many churches and refugee camps in that war-torn country.

After preaching for six weeks, as they were preparing to board the plane for home, Dwight was handed a note that questioned: "Do you only go to the healthy people now?"

They immediately deplaned, claimed their luggage, and returned to the leper colony. Dwight asked, "When do you want me to preach?"

The answer was, "Right now because some of us will not be here tomorrow." So he did.

Fergusons at the dedication of a new church in South Korea for son, Marvin.

He preached to people sitting on a cold, hard concrete floor. Many of the people sang *Amazing Grace* and other hymns of the church, even though they had no palates. Some of them were missing noses or ears or other body parts, but that did not keep them from worshiping the Lord. The congregation ignored the discomfort of the freezing weather with no heat.

During the days Dwight preached, many lepers placed their faith in Jesus Christ, and Dwight came home never to be the same. He could preach to thousands of people, give countless illustrations, and never lose his composure. However, when he preached and told about his experience in South Korea with the lepers, he could never tell it without shedding tears.

This was the Fergusons' first trip back to the leprosarium since the Korean War. Prior to their leaving the first time, the people of the leper community gave each of the Fergusons 24-karat gold rings with the inscription "You are Married to Us." On the return trip to South Korea which Velma and I led, the Fergusons wore those rings.

On the 1979 MFM trip, Dwight and Stella made themselves at home in the leper colony by sitting on two buckets turned upside down. The folks in the colony on this trip were busy making large amounts of kimchi in huge clay pots in the center of the colony, and the odors that permeated the whole colony from their personal hygiene was quite noticeable. The odors of garlic, onions, fish, etc. that filled the air did not bother the Fergusons. Dwight talked to them via an interpreter and reminisced about their earlier visit 25 years prior. When Dwight and Stella removed their rings and began passing them around, it was a precious time, with the lepers exclaiming, "You are not a legend, you really exist!"

The leper colony became a holy place that day because of two gold rings.

**See the Glossary for a description of the term doghouse.*

From a Shy Teenager to a Dreamer for Jesus

Steve Rollo

Introduction by Warren Hardig

"What is desirable in a man is his kindness" (Proverbs 19:22).

Steve Rollo is kind. His parents, along with every Rollo I know, are kind. Steve and I met when he invited me to be the missionary speaker for their church in Nelson, New Zealand. Steve could have "Get it Done" for a middle name, as the Men for Missions groups under his leadership in New Zealand have been men who do the work and finish projects. Steve's efforts have been blessed of the Lord, including some which were completed in closed countries and cannot be told here for safety reasons.

Steve is a great friend and brother; we have worked together on two continents. He reminded me of the old adage, "Whatever we want most will define our greatest prospects for joy." Steve finds his joy in Jesus. In his own words, here is his story…

I was blessed to be brought up in a Christian family in what many call one of the most beautiful parts of the world: Nelson, New Zealand. Nelson, surrounded by mountains and an ocean, has three national parks within a one-hour drive and hundreds of beautiful sandy beaches. Apart from my time on the mission field, I have lived my life within one kilometer of a beautiful beach.

My two younger brothers, an older sister, and I grew up with a very hard-working dad. He spent long hours not only working in business, but also fixing everything from fishing nets, clotheslines, playground equipment, wrought ironwork, security safes, and more. As the eldest son, I learned from my dad how to be hard working and creative, how to love fishing and help others.

When I was 14, my school, my parents and I all agreed that school wasn't my passion. A little before the legal age to leave, I left school to learn my father's trade as a locksmith, completing my apprenticeship before all my schoolmates even finished school. At 17, I took three months off work to travel the world alone. My first stop was Singapore. I then made my way to Scotland to visit some relatives on my father's side (my father's parents had migrated to New Zealand a few years before he was born). I also made a stop in the United States before returning home.

Although I had been brought up as a Christian and had been baptized at age 13, I spent most weekends hiking in the mountains, fishing, kayaking, or riding my motorcycle rather than attending church. I would mix working long hours with helping people and always enjoying the outdoors.

I appreciated having parents who brought us up knowing God and enjoying life. I will always remember the day when I was little that I told my mother I would be a missionary or a minister when I grew up. Little did I know that God was directing my steps. I didn't know then He would lead me to spend much of my adult life serving Him, first as a missionary and then as a minister.

At 18, I remember a rare Sunday going to church rather than the mountains, not knowing the speaker that day was the New Zealand Director of Men for Missions (MFM), who told of an opportunity to do some painting at Tokyo Bible Seminary. Wow, that sounded like an amazing opportunity! I had already developed a love to travel, and going to Asia sounded great.

Little did I imagine that going to Japan on an MFM team would change my life. Entirely.

Even before leaving for that adventure, God's hand was on my life. On the day I was supposed to leave Nelson, a major storm closed our airport and cancelled my flight to connect with our international flight. All packed and ready to leave, I assumed it wasn't possible to catch my flight to Japan.

A phone call from Air NZ asked if I would be willing to take a special flight direct from Nelson to Auckland (something unheard of, as all flights from Nelson went via our capital city, Wellington). Leaving on the same flight from Nelson was another couple from our church who were also heading on their first mission adventure, in the South Pacific nation of Vanuatu. Maybe it was their prayers that provided this direct flight for us to reach our international flight.

Arriving in Japan, I was hit with heat, culture shock, and food I didn't at first enjoy. We were greeted by a shed full of paint – and questions, such as "Why would you come from New Zealand to paint a school just as the rainy season started?" Yes, it was the rainy season, but thanks to another miracle from God, we had no rain during the three weeks we needed to complete the project.

I was still a shy teenager at that time, so another shock even greater than the culture shock, was to discover that I was expected to share my testimony at a local church on Sunday, something I had never considered before. But God provided the miracle of sending me to a small church with just a few members. I couldn't decide whether it was harder to have to stand and share in the service or to later sit and eat a big bowl of little fish for lunch. I still didn't fully understand Asian food. I loved catching fish, but I hadn't yet desired to eat it regularly.

The adventure of speaking through a translator was interesting, especially when there seemed to be no translation for explaining my occupation as a locksmith. The closest explanation was an honest burglar, can you imagine? I chuckled at that. I was amazed how just sharing about the miracle of getting a flight during a storm and arriving in Japan brought so much encouragement and interest to those listening in that little church.

While I struggled to finish my oversized bowl of crunchy little fish, I was challenged by the story of four young women who had been attacked and had their long hair cut off while they were singing and witnessing for Jesus! The attack didn't stop them. They continued to share their love for Jesus. I heard how that little church was the only Christian witness in a city of 250,000 people. I was stunned as I thought of the nearly 100 churches in my city of 40,000.

Just as we were finishing up that visit, a young guy arrived on his new motorcycle. This young man had heard some foreigners were visiting and he wanted to show off his motorcycle. Little did I know I would end up meeting this fellow again two years later in downtown Tokyo. Yes, it was a miracle because God had a journey ahead for the two of us. I had to wait 30 years to fully understand how that meeting would impact me – far beyond my imagination.

While walking through a local park that Sunday, I was confronted with a sight I never expected to see: I watched people bow to worship what appeared to be just a rock with a rope tied around it. Others nearby paid for a piece of paper with a prewritten prayer they placed on a tree. I had been raised knowing there was a living God who loved me and wanted me to talk to Him, not simply recite a prewritten prayer written by someone else. To me, God wasn't a small rock with a rope tied around it; my God was the creator of the heavens and the earth.

Our team may have transformed the look of the Tokyo Bible Seminary, but on that trip God transformed my life. As we traveled, we were told there was no Christian church or outreach for hours along the highway. My prayer quickly became: "God, send missionaries to Japan. God, please, may these beautiful people know You." Even before leaving Japan, I had a hunger to go back, but how could a locksmith (or an honest burglar!) from New Zealand tell people about Jesus and His love for them? I couldn't speak their language and I surely didn't like their food, but I had fallen in love with Japan.

One year later I was leading another Men for Missions team to work at the youth camp on Ōshima Island, Japan. I was no longer a shy teen who would choose to enjoy the outdoors rather than attend church. I was a teenager on fire. I needed people to understand that many were going to hell without hearing of God's lifesaving love.

I often wondered whether people understood that God was changing my life and filling it with a new passion for sharing the Gospel, or if they were just shocked to see a quiet teenager turn into the person being asked to preach in his church's evening outreaches.

I started to produce a missions letter encouraging prayer for missionaries, became the missions representative for our church, and led the challenge for our church to increase its missions giving. As our church started to grow, our missions and outreach budget expanded to 52 percent of our income.

The more I prayed for Japan and asked God to send missionaries to areas where people hadn't yet heard the Good News of Jesus, the stronger I felt Him saying, *Steve, what about you?*

But what could I do? I hadn't done well at school. In fact, I had left it with no interest in reading or studying. I spoke English but my grammar wasn't good, I never completed an exam while in school, and my first test was my driver's license test on my 15th birthday.

What would be required of me if I went?

With opportunities to speak in churches and Christian meetings, I found myself saying, *Here am I - but send Sam!* I knew God called many, but many had excuses. How could I be a missionary?

The more I prayed for Japan and its lost, the more God challenged me. I heard again and again: *Steve, I want you in Japan.*

I thought, *Okay, Lord, I will apply to OMS as a short-term missionary.* But it had to be to Japan.

During the application process, I had the opportunity to preach at a little rural community church about an hour and a half from my home. It was a service I will never forget. The organist sang her lungs out while she played, but at one point halfway through a hymn she decided to stop singing, so everyone else did. *What do I do now?* I wondered. I was quiet, really shy, with no vocal skills; I started singing, however, and led everyone else to join me. Thankfully the small congregation and the organist took the hint and started singing again, maybe just to drown out my singing.

During the following week, an older gentleman from that church visited me and handed me a large check. He had just sold part of his farm and felt God was telling him to give me the money toward my missionary support. I was amazed! I hadn't told anyone at that church I had applied to OMS for missionary service. He could have bought a new car (he traveled in a very old one), bought more land, or invested the money, but he obeyed God's voice and presented a check that covered 20 percent of my full support. I later heard this Christian man had fought in the Pacific theater against the Japanese soldiers during the war and had every right to be angry with the Japanese, but he chose instead to obey God.

With my church supplying a big portion of my needs, I had 70 percent of my support requirement before I was even accepted as a missionary candidate. I waited what seemed an interminable time to obtain a missionary visa to go to Japan, because at the time New Zealand and Japan didn't have good relations. I continued to visit churches nearby to share about the need for Christians to show love to those who had still had not heard the Gospel of Jesus Christ.

As the time for my departure approached, God introduced me to a cute young lady named Lynn who was working in our family business. It didn't take long before I asked her to marry me, knowing we would have a long, and long-distance, engagement. I wrote Lynn at least one letter every day I was in Japan, which often led to several letters arriving in her mailbox on the same day. She ended up with a sizable Japanese stamp collection, since she kept every letter she received.

I was reminded of God's guidance in our journey after traveling down the West Coast to speak in a Hokitika church the day following our engagement. I hadn't known then that Lynn's grandparents were involved as young Christians in building that church. I learned their story from my host family, who had purchased the farm from Lynn's grandparents. I found out I was staying on the very farm where Lynn's mother grew up. It is a small world, indeed!

After several long delays, I flew to the Japanese embassy in our capital city to see if there was another way to obtain a visa. They suggested I get a 90-day visa and simply renew it, rather than attempt a missionary or work visa. I eventually discovered that did not work, and I would have to leave Japan after being there only six months.

But after more wrangling over red tape, the day came when I flew to Japan to begin my missionary assignments. I worked at Tokyo Bible Seminary and Key Center English Center, and followed those up by working at the camp on Ōshima Island.

Every day in Japan increased my love for the people. To this day, I count it such a privilege to have been able to not only spend time in that country but to participate in building God's church there.

With visa problems six months into my 2½-year assignment and having a beautiful young lady awaiting my return, I made my way back to New Zealand. The theme of our wedding was "In His time everything becomes beautiful," because we trusted God by serving Him and committing to Him our future as husband and wife.

Our pastor suggested that Lynn and I spend our first year of marriage taking time out from full-time ministry, but he also asked whether we would lead a life group in our home and invited me to join our church's preaching roster. However, my passion for missions kept pulling at my heart. When I asked OMS how I could get involved with Men for Missions, they asked whether I would be willing to serve as an associate staff member. I didn't really know what that meant, but I took on the challenge of starting the first MFM Council at our home in New Zealand.

While working in our family business, I had found plenty of opportunities to be involved in helping in our community, serving in our church, and raising money for missions. As Lynn and I built our home, we had many opportunities to host visiting Japanese students. We also had two needy 13-year-old boys come to live with us, even having one boy's dad sleeping on our living room floor.

Our love for Asia provided an opportunity to return to Japan with MFM, then take a trip into seven Asian countries to look at possible mission opportunities. We talked excitedly about the potential, wondering where God would lead us.

My heart was heavy for the lost. I had a concern for the disadvantaged and wanted to help those who didn't have it easy; we saw many opportunities on our trip. We went to a Hong Kong refugee camp where thousands of people were locked up, visited slums in Thailand including a ministry that ministered to children whose mothers were in Thai prisons, and toured an orphanage in Macau – the world's most densely populated colony at the time, and an area rife with crime and drug problems.

Lynn and I returned home, burdened with the thought of homeless children in countries that offered them little hope. We grappled with the challenge of figuring out where we could help the most.

Working in our family business allowed me time to work with MFM, and it wasn't long before I was invited to become the New Zealand director of MFM. As we prayed, God blessed us with the news that Lynn was expecting our first child. God was telling us we needed more experience with children before we could consider being involved with an orphanage in Asia. God blessed us with four sons – Joshua, Phillip, Benjamin, and Campbell. We now have the added blessing of two daughters-in-law, and, as I write this, we are about to be blessed with our first grandchild.

Having hosted many exchange students, working as State Chaplain in a state-run school, and starting children's and youth ministries, I still wonder if God is continuing to train us. Regardless of God's reasons, we continued forward.

In the early days of our marriage, God provided many opportunities to help raise money for missions. For several years our passion was cooking and enjoying food, so we started catering for functions, which provided funds for missions projects. It was also a good way to share about missions; as we provided good food, we always shared our hearts with those we were serving.

Even in the early days of starting New Zealand's first MFM Council, God began providing more opportunities to help overseas. A large cyclone had hit Solomon Island near New Zealand with a force that almost wiped it out, and we were able to send three large teams in succession to help with rebuilding. The country had very little, and most of its resources had been wiped out, so all the teams had to be fully self-sufficient with their supplies, food, and tools. We shared this need with the media and quickly had more than a ton of supplies donated. Our next challenge was to ask the airline if we could take a literal ton of luggage with our team! God opened the door and amazingly all the extra luggage was allowed at no additional cost.

The first chance to help after the cyclone hit brought even more opportunities. We helped put water resources into villages, assisted with many building projects, and accepted an invitation to extend a church building in Samoa, which we did every year to accommodate the growing congregation of believers. We even converted an illegal nightclub into a school. Every project needed a team, and we always had people willing to take the job.

Since opportunities for fundraising projects kept appearing, we started a second New Zealand MFM Council in Motueka, a smaller town 50 kilometers from our city. This provided joint fundraising events and new members joining MFM teams; also in time, it produced short-term missionaries and New Zealand's new OMS director.

One of the best opportunities the Nelson MFM Council had was to sell Christmas trees. Nelson is surrounded by hills that are great for the forestry industry. Around Christmas, we gathered into groups in the evening and headed into the forests to cut pine trees that self-grew amongst the planted trees. We took those trees to a local market, or just stood on street corners and sold them. We raised thousands of dollars to help with projects like building a church in India, providing furniture in Bible schools, and building water wells and pumps.

Our Nelson Council maintained a steady income by collecting fowl manure from a local poultry farm, plus growing and selling potatoes, arranging fairs, introducing folks to *hangis* (a Maori-style meal cooked on hot rocks), and hosting BBQs. The Nelson Council was also known for printing and selling writing pads with Scripture.

A high-profile fundraising project God provided emerged after a large retail building alongside our own family business caught fire and burned down. After the site was cleared, we asked the building owner if we could rent the site. With their permission we turned it into a parking lot and rented space to local businesses.

With two councils growing well, we added a third in Waikato in North Island. God continued to provide projects and opportunities to send teams, always with people eager and ready to join those teams.

Many trips required long and expensive air travel, so we looked for new opportunities in new countries, especially ones closer to New Zealand. Teams went to the Solomon Islands, Samoa, Fiji, Tonga, and Papua New Guinea. Opportunities started to come from Asia. We Kiwis, who are known to be adventurous, were given some exciting new ministry opportunities in Asia. Teams for our China Bike project opened doors for many as we joined with Asian ministries in areas accessible only by mountain bike.

Many of our prayer teams went into closed countries, which helped stir a hunger for Jesus in many people. One team who visited an isolated mountain area left a Bible with a schoolteacher. When we returned a year later, we discovered the teacher had dedicated his life to Jesus and was now using that Bible as he taught. Only God knows how many will join us in glory as a result of teams who used their opportunities through MFM to share Jesus.

One team in Asia took a very long train trip that required them to be on the train overnight. Our team leader was awakened by a man very close to his face, and was startled and frightened until he heard the simple words, “I want to know your God.” After quickly waking up the translator, they shared the Good News of Jesus with the man. It didn’t take long for the man to open his heart and ask for forgiveness. Before the end of the train ride, 10 passengers had given their hearts to Jesus, including one who was led to the Lord by the man who had just become a Christian.

When I look back on some of the adventures and testimonies of teams who went to places where people don’t usually go, I recognize God opens doors beyond our imagination. He always goes before us and opens hearts.

On one trip I was randomly separated from my group by the airline and was seated in the back area of the plane with what turned out to be a group of government and businesspeople from a country we had been praying for. Through a translator, I had the privilege of talking and sharing with members of this group, including a government official who moved to the seat behind me.

“You can ask any question about my country,” he said. I took him up on the offer.

We also met a business leader who owned a chain of hotels, one of which our team would be staying in a week later. We met in her office on a later occasion.

During that flight, a lady on our team started sharing with a young man who was returning home. As soon as she started to share about Jesus, the man said he knew that his grandmother had been praying for him. Those prayers were answered on that flight as he gave his heart to Jesus. What a joy to meet with him a few days later and give him a Bible in his own language, in a country where Bibles aren't freely available!

Besides doing outreach, our teams were often available as couriers who could safely take many bags of books, teaching materials, and personal items into areas where they could be safely given out to whoever could use them most. I will never forget one trip when we arrived at customs with lots of luggage filled with Bibles and Christian literature we knew would be confiscated if they found them. All the customs officers were down at one end of the building as one of our team members placed his baggage on the security check table. I told him not to worry and to keep moving, fully expecting we would be stopped. One customs officer looked up and simply waved.

Wow, when God goes before us, what an experience!

At another border, the lady who had led the man on our flight to Jesus was stopped, and a number of immigration officers gathered to look at her passport. As team leader, I went over to check to see what was happening. We could not speak their language, so it was a little disconcerting; however, I soon understood they just wanted to know the lady's age. She was a very tall woman in her 70s with long, thick grey hair. They treated her as someone very important and wanted to look after her.

Another time, while with a prayer team, we were being shown around a park when I noticed a glow and graciousness in our guide. I also observed she was wearing a necklace with a cross. I asked our translator to ask whether she was a believer. The translator was hesitant, because it was highly unlikely she was a believer, telling us it was common for people in this area to wear jewelry that displayed a cross. After several requests, the translator finally asked, and the park guide confirmed what I had been sensing – yes, this lady was a Christian.

We explained we were visiting her country to encourage people with the Good News of the Gospel, and she shared what her life was like. She didn't know of any other Christians, or even whether there was a safe place to worship in the area. It was a great joy to be able to pray with her and leave her the gift of a Bible in her own language.

Our hearts were full of compassion for people in the countries we could visit, and we encouraged others to pray for the minority groups. We chose to pray for minority groups in two different countries – China and Indonesia – in an area we understood to be the most Muslim-concentrated area, an area with almost no Christians.

A new focus in our meetings was to encourage prayer for these minority groups. It was such a privilege to be able to encourage prayer teams to visit these locations. Little did I know that 25 years later I would meet a lady from one of the Chinese minority groups on an isolated beach in Vanuatu, a small country in the Pacific.

Remember that couple from my home church who left Nelson on that special God-arranged flight following the storm that almost caused me to miss my first MFM adventure? Ron and his wife, Janet, not only visited Vanuatu that year, but fell in love with that country and its people, who are said to be the friendliest people on earth. Ron, a builder by trade, oversaw the building of a number of projects, including Ranwadi High School, one of the larger boarding schools in Vanuatu, as well as some church buildings and hostels. Ron has visited

Vanuatu most years since, even following the passing of his wife. Ron and I were connected through my late father; my father and he had been close friends, and Ron had always wanted my father to go to Vanuatu with him. Sadly, my dad was never able to go with him, but I had the opportunity to join Ron on several ministry teams to Vanuatu.

One such opportunity was to join Ron and a team from Motueka to build a community center. The day before we returned to New Zealand, we visited one of Vanuatu's beautiful sandy beaches. While the rest of the group was out around the coral reef, I was just enjoying the warm water when an Asian lady swam over to talk. I learned in this interaction that sometimes God sends people to us. This lady was from China, and when she saw a picture of another Pacific island country, Fiji, she decided to travel there. On her journey, she discovered other Pacific countries, including Vanuatu, and had read about this beautiful beach roughly an hour from the nearest town with accommodations. She met someone who offered to let her stay, and ironically visited the beach the same day and time we did. Amazingly, she was from the very people's group I had been praying for over the past 30 years. Wow! Thank you, Lord, for allowing that privilege!

The lady mentioned she would appreciate a ride into the town, as she found the isolation overwhelming. We were happy to offer her a ride and were eager to learn as much as we could about her culture. This led to asking if she had heard of Jesus, and she said she had not. What an opportunity to share Jesus with someone from the very group I had encouraged others to start praying for.

This was an unlikely opportunity on an island a mere three-hour flight from my own country but a world away from this lady's home. I got to share about Jesus and His love and teach her how to pray to a God who loves her so much.

Imagine the joy when she visited us in New Zealand a year later, along with her husband and brother-in-law. It was an even greater privilege to have them visit the church I now pastor and to get the opportunity to show them the beauty of our country while continuing to share the Good News.

That initial meeting in Vanuatu was arranged by God, and it reminds me of other meetings only God could have arranged.

Two years after meeting the young man who came to that first Japanese church I visited, we were surprised to see each other in Tokyo. How amazing that such things can happen in a city of over 36,000,000 people! We became friends during my time in Japan, but over time our friendship faded and we lost contact with each other. It wasn't until about five years ago I received a Facebook message that read, "Is this Steve Rollo, the rocksmith in New Zealand?" I remembered how the Japanese struggle to pronounce the letter *L*, and smiled when I realized he meant "locksmith." I told him it was me, his old friend, but I was no longer a locksmith, having now become a pastor of a church.

Every now and again we messaged each other, but it was just a casual friendship. Two years ago, I sent him a message to wish him a happy birthday. A bit of time passed before I got a reply from his daughter, on his behalf. He had awakened on his birthday to discover he was paralyzed from the chest down. He could no longer walk and had very little movement. The doctors found some cancer that attached to his spine and had paralyzed him. He was very distressed and didn't want to continue his life. He was incapable of doing much, and knew the cancer would take his life, anyway.

I replied and explained again I was now a pastor. I told him I believed in miracles and shared about all of the people who had been healed by Jesus. I told him our church would pray for him.

He had several tough treatments and struggled with depression. I sent him regular messages to encourage him and tell him we were still praying for healing. I so longed to be with him and lay hands on him, but we faithfully prayed. Several months later I received a strange message displaying a man's foot with his big toe moving. He followed the video with the words, "Steve, could this be your Jesus?"

He then told about a dream his daughter and granddaughter had of Jesus (whom they didn't know). I quickly replied "Yes!" and told him it was Jesus, and he better start believing in a miracle!

Today he is cancer free and goes walking, sometimes even running, with his family. Most importantly, he believes in Jesus, and his family does, too. Who said we can't reach people for Jesus when we are still at home? Through a chance meeting on an MFM trip over 40 years ago, God started a journey that would save a life and bring an entire family into God's love.

With the birth of our fourth son, I realized it was unfair to Lynn for me to be away as much I was. I had been visiting different churches, sharing about MFM. With sadness, I stepped down from my position with MFM, although I continued encouraging churches to send mission teams, especially bicycle teams, into Asian countries. For more than 20 years, two churches have been faithful in sending teams each year.

I continued to also work in our family locksmith business that had now expanded into retail. We began selling outdoor camping gear and became one of our country's largest suppliers of kayaks. Our business also included a store that sold BBQ equipment. I loved selling and loved working with the public, and when I found an opportunity to help someone we did.

The year I turned 40 things started to change. On my 40th birthday, a friend made me a walking stick as a joke, insinuating I was getting old. Maybe 40 wasn't that old yet, but one day when I wasn't feeling well my trip to the doctor's office turned into a trip to the hospital. I remember my doctor saying, "Steve, you may just have the flu, but I want you to go to the hospital now."

He didn't tell me, but he saw signs that my health wasn't good and my heart was in bad shape. I went from being a happy businessman to a patient waiting to be airlifted to Wellington for urgent open-heart surgery. I underwent triple bypass surgery, and the recovery was full of setbacks.

A few days after surgery both of my lungs collapsed. I was put on life support, and I remember praying, "Lord, I trust You. If you want me there with You, that's okay. If I can say, however, I would rather spend more time with my family."

The next thing I remember was waking up in intensive care with doctors in amazement at how successfully I had come through the surgery. Many across the globe were praying for me, and God still had some projects for me.

Three weeks later I was allowed to fly home. I soon realized things didn't always go well during surgery when they were trying to reconnect bones. A medical mishap summed it up.

The surgeons tried to hold my bones together with a lot of wires, but as I began to heal, I experienced unbelievable pain. I could feel my bones moving. I had very little movement in my arms, and soon wires started to break, as did the wires holding my sternum and ribs. I had to have another surgery to remove the broken wires, but my bones didn't want to join. After weeks of recovery, I returned to work, only to find the pain getting worse. Ultimately, I made the decision to give up working for a while to recover and spend more time with my family.

As I was able, I volunteered as a parent helper at our local school. They asked me to come on staff as school chaplain, which was unusual in a state primary school. I agreed to come on staff, but not in a paid position. As I began serving as school chaplain, I chuckled to realize that just when my boys were leaving school, I went back. I would tell students I had the best job in the school, since my job was to make sure everyone was happy. So, if anyone wasn't happy, they talked to me.

Through serving as school chaplain, I had so many opportunities to continue being Jesus' light in our community. The passion to do more for Jesus continued to grow, leading me into a part-time position as pastor of a nearby church, and 15 years later, I continue to serve as a pastor at the Richmond Church of Christ.

As pastor, my passion for the lost and disadvantaged is stronger than ever. While the church I pastor is made up mostly of older people, we aim to see it become a church of all ages reaching our community for Jesus.

Through school chaplaincy and being available to help those in need, I've had an interesting ministry that reaches many. It isn't uncommon to find me ministering in areas well beyond my natural abilities – like helping a solo dad who was involved with a major drug dealer, or ministering to a man who, although he fought with his ex-wife, later turned his life around and asked to be baptized.

Another opportunity was to share Jesus with a former gang member who lived in a shantytown near Nelson. This man, a former Rastafarian, was well over 6'6" with dreadlocks that hung below his waist and a back full of gang tattoos. What a privilege it was to baptize him as he changed his life to follow Jesus. Sadly, a few months later, he drowned in a flooded river near where he still lived in a tent. I was asked to bless his campsite and perform his funeral. At the end of the funeral, two of his friends asked to be baptized in the same river where he had drowned.

My journey has been that of a shy teenager who joined an MFM team going to Japan, to someone who dreamed of what God can do when we make ourselves available, who dreams he can do more, and who still dreams of the day when in glory someone stops and says, "Steve, thank you for praying. Thank you for helping me find Jesus."

My wife Lynn says I dream too much, while others claim I am a man of vision – but I am just someone who loves Jesus. When you love Jesus, you just have to tell others about His amazing love. You can't help it!

Recently a pastor from Kenya challenged all pastors to, in his words, "have at least 10 prayers that make Jesus sweat." After searching for what one of my prayers could be, I am challenged to pray for the privilege of baptizing a thousand people within the next 10 years – a crazy prayer since in the past 10 years I have only baptized about 100. I love Jesus and believe in His power. Some may say it's a dream, but I believe that by July 2029 I will see more than a thousand people baptized in Jesus' name.

By the way, I have only 997 to go. Will you join me and pray for miracles in Jesus? Will you join me in this prayer that can only happen in God's power?

I am simply a man who went on an MFM team and had my life transformed, but I learned how much Jesus loves me and I must let others know. When God's love gets hold of you, even a shy teenager will find a way to share that amazing love with others!

The Dependability of God

Warren Hardig

We can learn about God's dependability by reading His Word and experiencing it through the Holy Spirit. Another way is by His living in the heart of a fellow believer, the same Holy Spirit who raised Jesus from the dead. He lives in the heart of every believer and can testify to our spirit. That's why it is so important to be able to give a testimony of God working in your life.

Our heart is the control panel of our personality. If Jesus is in our heart, we need to act like it. When we embrace the Spirit of the living Lord and testify of His goodness, He will, at different times, reward us with friendships more precious than any earthly wealth.

When missionaries began coming to our home or we met them at the Broken Heart Club meetings, I wondered how they could have enough faith to rely on God to supply their needs through people like me. How could God supply my commitments for extra income when I knew my projected salary? My first Faith Promise (the concept of trusting God to give through me above and beyond what He has given to me, such as my salary) was $100.

In less than two months, He gave me five crisp $20 bills out of the blue. I was amazed!

I depend on God for protection. During one of our adventures, Velma, Roger, and I were traveling home on the interstate. We pulled off to find a motel room, a rare thing for us since we almost always stayed with friends in their homes. We purposely passed the first motel and decided we would stop to eat, then go to the second motel on the exit for our stay. When we walked into the lobby of that second motel and looked over to the first one, we saw several police cars with their lights flashing brightly.

I asked, "What is going on?"

The answer was, "They just had an armed robbery." Had we stopped there, we would have been in the middle of that robbery.

Joining the Men for Missions staff meant beginning with a salary that totaled less than the withholding from our previous employers, so we had no idea how we would live on that amount. We also had to raise double our salary to cover our ministry costs, like rent, utilities, travel expenses, and other costs. Living in the Midwest, we had many friends in agriculture who were experiencing tough times. They were living by faith as much as or more than we were. We all trusted the Lord together and depended on His provision.

We had seen many miracles in the lives of our support team. When we began deputation, I asked God for five prayer supporters to every one financial supporter, which was perhaps the best decision I ever made in MFM. We have hundreds of friends, and I believe all of them have prayed and continue to pray for us. We have been fortunate to receive many gifts that make us cry, from a dozen eggs to a recurring donation of 50 cents a month. So many made sacrifices to bless our ministry. God is dependable. He's been with me all over the world.

During my travels, one thing I tried to avoid when visiting a church for the first time was Sunday school. I cannot count the number of times I have heard the teacher say, "You are going to have to help me this morning because I did not have time to study this week." Perhaps lack of prayer and preparation by those who are teaching contributes to our culture changing the church rather than the church changing our culture.

God is dependable. The history of what started out as the Oriental Missionary Society, now One Mission Society, is filled with miracles of how faithful and dependable God is.

When Velma and I joined the MFM staff, one part of our training was a continuation of what we had learned by experience in the Broken Heart Club: Be prepared through prayer. When I started working in my region, we would pray through the miles of a road trip; we prayed for the missionaries of every country, which was just a part of our DNA. Prayer was key to everything. The Holy Spirit can direct you to the right Scripture and help you recollect events and remember names. He is more dependable than I could ever describe. He is concerned about the little things of life that help us with our witness and credibility.

On one trip to Wisconsin, I visited the home and farm of a young couple who welcomed me for their evening meal. They were very attentive to my presentation of Men for Missions. When my host went to the barn the next morning, I pulled on my jeans, shirt and boots then went out to feed the calves with him. Later we cleaned out some of the stalls in the barn. I had time until my next meeting, which was with the president of a major corporation in Milwaukee. I wasn't far from where he lived in Milwaukee and he didn't arrive home until around 5:30 p.m., so I used my time to scoop ground feed and clean stalls in the barn … and get calf manure on my jeans.

In the late afternoon I bathed and changed from boots and jeans to wing tips and my best suit, white shirt, and tie. Needless to say, this stop was with folks high on the social ladder, and I was concerned about my ability to communicate and motivate them toward foreign missions.

My hosts were warm, wonderful, evangelical Christians. We talked about Haiti and other countries. They had been on a Caribbean cruise and met our field treasurer, Kent VanDervort, in Haiti. That was how I came to be in their home. After dinner, we went into the living room for a very pleasant conversation. Somehow, it turned to what we do in some of our leisure time. We were pleasantly surprised to learn we both had a love for over-and-under shotguns, and we both had German shorthaired hunting dogs.

The next morning, as my host went to his downtown office and I left to visit some folks in Iowa, we agreed to stay in touch – and we did.

God can and does help with relationships. He is dependable. After my meeting with the corporate president, I always traveled the region with jeans, boots, and a suit and wing tips. If no one else was with me on the trip, I spent most of my time praying because I had only God to depend on, but He has never failed me. We can put Him to any test, but we dare not tempt Him. Too many people try to play "Let's Make a Deal" with God. For instance, I met a guy in Colorado who said that once he started making $50,000 a year, then he would begin tithing. God calls us to be faithful no matter how much or how little we have.

We can go anywhere God leads to fulfill the Great Commission and He is fully dependable. One of my favorite regions of the world to take ministry teams is the South Pacific because of the different cultures, different dress, and different foods – and multitudes of people for whom Jesus shed His blood and gave His life. Many worship gods with no hope. They sacrifice money, food, and anything of value to appease an idol.

Hong Kong became one of my favorite places. I love the hustle and bustle of the city-country, the view from the peak, the night market, and the shopping for bargains. In one of the OMS-related churches near the New Territories, I met the secretary of the Hong Kong Stock Exchange, who was supportive of opening a Men for Missions office there. He did not encourage us to start at that time, stating the one thing that motivates people in Hong Kong was greed – so if we could not help them worship an idol, our mission would not be openly welcome.

One of my dreams that did not materialize was opening a Men for Missions International office in Singapore. The logistics of such a move were too much for OMS in those days. But I have always enjoyed meeting businessmen all over the world. I became friends with a lawyer and his brother in the Philippines; I also made friends with a church leader in Indonesia. Dick Capin, another southern Illinois businessman, started a Men for Missions office in South Korea in 1962. Dick was still active into his 90s, working with the Billy Graham Evangelistic Association.

Bill and Joyce Oden, OMS missionaries in the Philippines, started a church in Manila. They were instrumental in reaching not only those who were economically challenged but also many upper-class individuals. One of those was Helen Vela, a very popular late-night television talk show host. She had Bill and Joyce on her program, which meant they were reaching people on their way home after a night of partying.

One time I was leading an MFM ministry team at a church in Manila on a Sunday. That day, they were commissioning Helen to go to China, and the news of her presence in the church brought a huge crowd to the service. Bill graciously gave his pulpit to me for the morning message. It seemed so ironic to me that I, a southern Illinois businessman, should speak to a TV personality and others of all classes.

When I finished my testimony and remarks, I invited anyone who wanted to have their sins forgiven to please come forward and kneel at the altar. The altar was full of seekers. Bill and the elders of the church began praying with those who came forward. I went to a man in the back area of the church because there wasn't room for him at the altar. I prayed and listened as two elders talked with him. They knew he was a producer of pornography and was far from God. He prayed, and we all prayed with him.

Again, God proved that He is dependable. I was in over my head. I was a common guy talking about a wonderful Savior to people of another land and culture. God has never failed me.

Dependency on God gave our staff so many miracles during the 1990s. In the years OMS was a part of the CoMission,* we expected at least a miracle a day. I cannot write about a lot of miracles for a couple of reasons: First, you would think me a religious nut if I wrote about some encounters that took place with the supernatural in different countries. Second, where marriages or families have been in trouble then restored, my lips are sealed. I would never embarrass my friends.

God is faithful and more wonderful than I could ever describe. He is totally dependable. I have found that it takes more faith to be in business than to be a missionary. While I was employed in the farm chemical business, I discovered there was a daily struggle that frequently involved employers and customers wanting me to make decisions that, as a Christian, I found to be immoral. Every Christian, whether layman, clergy, or missionary, needs to practice certain disciplines to discourage Satan's attack on our lives. It's not that we might lose our salvation if we don't, it's rather the importance of having an intimacy with God that lets you clearly hear what He wants you to do. My purpose is to be constantly marinated in God's Word, and be faithful to keep my prayer life vigilant for the Kingdom of God.

Scripture declares that the Lord "is a friend who sticks closer than a brother" (Proverbs 18:24), so why don't we trust Him for more?

**See the Glossary for a description of CoMission.*

The Man Whose Clothes Were Not Good Enough for Him to be Saved

Warren Hardig

In the early 1980s, the U.S. MFM Cabinet had its semi-annual meeting in Port-au-Prince, Haiti, where we sat at tables around the pool at Villa Ormiso. This new location was a huge change from our typical locations, such as church fellowship halls and motel conference rooms. Our two days of business stretched into five and the last item of business was voted on by a ballot passed down the aisle of a 757 airplane on our flight back to Miami.

We had briefly gone shopping with our wives and visited various cultural places in Port-a-Prince. One day we divided into four teams of eight and went into the communities to do door-to-door evangelism. Our team leader, Dr. Harold Brown, oversaw the OMS work in Haiti.

At one point, our evangelism team was welcomed into a large but very modest hut. Harold explained to the people there in Creole that we were Christians who wanted to tell them about Jesus. He asked the seven or eight people if they were Christians, and two or three people gave positive confirmation; the remaining people in the group left the hut through an opening in the side. Those folks were replaced by many other curious people who came into the hut to hear more.

One man in particular drew my attention. He was kneeling on the ground about 18 inches in front of me and busily sharpening his machete on a flat stone. His machete lay close to my foot.

I asked Gladys Gaskell from Horton, Kansas, if she would sing a song. She and her husband, Dave, were in the bolt manufacturing business and attended the Methodist church in Horton where Gladys sang specials on a regular basis.

Dave and Gladys were not strangers to Haiti or to Men for Missions. Dave served on the associate staff and worked with me in Kansas. He had made seven trips to Haiti, and on most of those trips, he helped build churches. Dave and his brother, Tom, were benevolent in the Lord's work.

Their business, Gaskell Bolt Company, was the meeting place for the MFMers to prefabricate metal churches out of scrap steel they found in the area. Neighbors who heard of the project (and, I suspect, the homemade ice cream they served) came on the designated evenings and Saturdays to fabricate the structure of a church; later Dave and other men traveled to Haiti to erect the church and put on the finishing touches. Subsequently, that project got them involved in another church, and another, and another.

Dave had an astounding faith. While they were putting a roof on a church near Cap Haitien in the blazing sun, he suggested to his fellow workers that they pray for cloud cover. Within 15 minutes, a cloud covered the blazing sun and remained for the rest of the day. "We don't trust the Lord enough," said Dave.

When the group found enough scrap steel to fabricate 11 more churches, Dave and the MFMers went to Haiti and put them together. Only our Lord knows the number of people who have been blessed by these men with Dave at the helm. What an incredible investment of a life!

On that day in the Haitian hut where I asked Gladys to sing, she gladly agreed. Gladys had always sung with accompaniment, but that day there were no instruments. Despite the lack of accompaniment, Gladys' beautiful singing quickly attracted more people.

I went through The Roman Road* with our curious audience and had one of our team members give his testimony. Then I spoke from Titus 3:3-7. Throughout it all I kept watching the gentleman sharpening his machete on the ground in front of my feet. After my exhortation from Titus, he said, “My clothes aren’t good enough to accept Jesus.”

I responded, “I had manure on my clothes the morning I accepted Jesus.” There was no need to try to explain the difference between manure and commercial fertilizer, it was a true statement.

Not saying a word, the gentleman laid down his machete, stood up, went out the side opening, and walked into the hut next door. He was gone for a couple of minutes and then reappeared in clean clothes. He came back in through the same entrance, circled around behind me, and came to my right side. Kneeling down in the dirt, he extended his left hand and I firmly held it in my own and knelt with him. My new friend and brother repented of his sins and asked Jesus to come into his life. The dirt floor of that hut in rural Haiti indeed became holy ground.

In His great graciousness, Jesus never requires us to go fix anything about ourselves and come back to Him. He is always, *always* ready for us whenever we come to Him, regardless of what is happening in our lives. Yet I appreciated the dignity and honor this man wanted to bring to the Lord.

Haiti, the poorest country in the Western Hemisphere, is a place where many North American lives have been changed by experiences with Haitians, like this man who believed his clothes weren’t good enough. Mine included.

**For The Roman Road, See Appendix A*

Christ Has Opportunities Galore for Me

Bruce Kelly

"The fruit of the righteous is a tree of life, and he who is wise wins souls" (Proverbs 11:30).

Introduction by Warren Hardig

It has been my privilege to be in the home of Bruce and Jan Kelly several times, yet it has not been often enough. I miss their smiles, their kindness, and most of all, their serious pursuit of Jesus.

I have heard it said, "If God doesn't have all of your heart, you will be frustrated trying to follow Him. He must be your passionate priority."

In his testimony below, Bruce alludes to my question, "What is the most important question in all the world for you?" For me, it's "What will happen when you die?"

My second question is, "What brings you the most joy in life?" For me, it's to see someone receive Christ as their Savior.

What brings *you* the most joy in life?

Jesus is Bruce's passionate priority. I love the Aussies. I hope you will be challenged and blessed by Bruce's testimony.

It all began on a sheep farm in Northern Victoria, Australia, where I lived with my parents and was struggling with teenage issues.

One evening, when the night sky was inky black and the atmosphere unpolluted, I said, "God, I do not know who You are, but if You're there, please help me." My prayer was answered the very next evening when a traveling evangelist led me to Christ during a visit to a neighbor's house. The following morning, I felt like I was walking on air with a spiritual bath on the inside. I can trace a change in the direction of my life back to that very moment.

My decision, however, created an uproar at home. My mother angrily demanded to know why a law-abiding youngster like me would get mixed up with what she called *that crazy religious rubbish*. "It'll drive you mad!" she shouted.

I had never seen her so angry. My parents refused me permission to associate with those neighbors. They burned Christian literature that was mailed to me, and they refused to allow me to attend church. That situation continued for 10 years. I survived in my faith by listening to Theodore Epp's "Back to the Bible" and Billy Graham's "Hour of Decision" radio programs late at night. Years later I told my story to J. Oswald Sanders, a world-famous missionary, statesman, and renowned author. I was hoping for sympathy, but his reply shook me. All he said was, "You've had a good education, haven't you?" I eventually understood this comment to be the best one-sentence counseling session I ever had.

One day I was shearing sheep when my mother, who must have been aware of my discontent, said, "There is a police recruiting campaign in town." A police career was not even a small blip on my radar screen. My only thought was, *Great! I can get out of this rotten shearing shed for an hour.* But to my shock, horror, and astonishment, this panel of high-ranking police officers selected me!

One of those officers was a devout Presbyterian. The panel gave all of the applicants a spelling list, which included the word "Presbyterian." I was the only one of 14 who knew how to spell it, which was the turning point that earned me a 25-year police career.

I drove home that afternoon wondering what I had gotten myself into, and my concern proved well founded. As a newly graduated police officer, I saw things that deeply shocked me. Not even in my wildest dreams could I imagine such things happening. If I had known of the unimaginable challenges I would face in those early years, I probably would not have enlisted. But in retrospect, I am deeply grateful for God's help for the survival of this socially deprived, green-behind-the-ears country boy.

Police service taught me much about God, others, and myself. I am still trying to process some of those earlier lessons wisely. My church attendance began when I left home for training at the police academy in Melbourne. Coincidentally, I met my wife, Jan, at the Scots Presbyterian Church not far from police HQ at that time. She had a Christian family upbringing and a farming heritage. We married over 55 years ago and have three adult children and four grandchildren. I am continually astonished by God's provision of this wonderful wife who supported me, especially during difficult episodes in both my police and Christian pursuits.

As the years rolled on, Jan and I became members of the Blackburn North Baptist Church, now known as the NewHope Baptist Church. There we were given copies of the OMS Outreach magazine which we enjoyed reading, but never sensed God's leading to the ministries that were discussed therein. This changed in February 1982 when Dr. Ed Kilbourne preached at one of our evening services.

His electric message sparked our interest in Men for Missions. That same evening, we met David Little, then Australian National Director of MFM, and his wife, Trish. Following several discussions with David and Trish, and after much prayer, we signed on for our first MFM tour to Indonesia and have returned twice since. Our teenage daughter and I later embarked on a six-week mission tour to India with OMS-New Zealand.

That first tour was especially meaningful to us. Our feet had barely touched the ground in Malang, East Java, when Adrian Morley, an Australian OMS missionary, swept us into a whirlwind of activity specially organized for our group's benefit. For six breathtaking, life-changing days, we participated with national Christians and missionaries in worship services, prayer meetings, and many discussions.

Don and Peggy Saum, the delightful American missionary couple who hosted us, went to great lengths to make us feel at home. Don, then dean of students and coordinator of practical ministries at the OMS Bible Seminary in Malang, still sends us regular news updates. We gratefully acknowledge their loving care, hospitality, and prayers, and continue to follow them with prayerful interest.

Soon after our arrival in Malang, Don acquainted us with the activities of local nightwatchmen homeowners who were hired to patrol their streets and properties. Each hour, on the hour, the nightwatchman would patrol the streets in his care and strike a large steel pipe suspended from a tree with his own metal rod. He struck the pipe at every hour to indicate the time: one strike for 1 a.m., two strikes for 2 a.m., and so on. This deafening noise assured his employer that his nightwatchman was on the job, and also deterred criminal activity.

The nightwatchman outside our bedroom window always seemed to strike first and loudest, followed by nightwatchmen in other areas.

Within seconds, gongs rang out in the still night air, some near and loud, others faint in the distance. The "sounding gong" turned my thoughts to Paul's comments in 1 Thessalonians 1:8: "From you the Word of the Lord has sounded forth not only in Macedonia and Achaia but also in every place." I am reminded thereby to pray for our missionaries, and sound out the Gospel at every opportunity.

Warren Hardig, John McLaughlin, and others from MFM were always welcome in our home. One morning when Warren was leading a devotional group in our home, he asked, "What is the most important question in all the world for you?" Aha! This was the sharp point I was searching for in my testimony. This question has since been incorporated hundreds of times in my testimony on city streets.

In my 45-year connection with OMS, the work of MFM councils was, in my opinion, the golden era of OMS in Australia. When David Little resigned his position, the directorship of MFM Australia fell on my shoulders. The grief of David's departure, coupled with the weight of my police duties and family responsibilities, brought about my resignation from national directorship. I still grieve the loss of MFM ministry here. However, we remain connected to OMS Australia.

Most of the above-mentioned missional activities occurred during my 25-year tenure with the police department. My four-year lecturing stint with police recruits at the Police Training Academy was a highlight which helped me overcome my fear of public speaking. I learned to present the information in the classroom so even the weakest student could understand, and to speak loud enough for the student in the far corner to hear. I was therefore able to be heard and understood by all, principles that assist both in testimony and preaching. They were good lessons learned at the taxpayers' expense.

Once while performing duties at a suburban police station, I was assigned duty at the Commonwealth Heads of Government Meeting (CHOGM). I unsuccessfully tried hard to get out of that assignment. I was in a rebellious period, not disposed to thank God for anything. Upon my arrival at CHOGM, my duties included the security of a railway overpass across a freeway. I was responsible for checking the rail tracks, drains, and sewers under and over the freeway for explosive devices. The first night was wet and cold. A car had careened out of control and brought high voltage power lines down around me, plunging the area into pitch blackness with traffic bearing down. My not being electrocuted or struck by an approaching vehicle was truly a miracle of God's grace.

Sergeant Bruce Kelly

Previously, Jan had confided my struggle with her Bible Study Fellowship leader. The group leader sent me a message using the acronym for the Commonwealth Heads of Government Meeting, CHOGM. Using those letters, he changed the meaning to "**C**hrist **H**as **O**pportunities **G**alore for **M**e." During this episode, the Lord challenged me to assist some of my colleagues in their spiritual struggles. Looking back, I understood why I was selected for CHOGM duty and once again praised God!

During my police tenure, the Rev. Dr. Graeme Smith conducted a two-year Bethel Bible study course at the NewHope Baptist Church. I enrolled because I wanted a better grasp of God's word. In the course, Genesis 12:1-3 provided a glimpse of God's unfolding drama of redemption, beginning before time began. This significant key released me from a reluctance to study Scripture, especially the Old Testament, and inspired a deeper walk in my spiritual pilgrimage. Church planting and street evangelism activities arose out of this revelation.

Upon retirement from the police department in 1987, after serving 25 years, I embarked on a 12-month training course for church planters with the Baptist Union of Victoria. During this course, the Lord moved us away from our home church to begin a church-planting ministry.

Our first appointment was in a rural area east of Melbourne where attendance soon reached some 80 people. Three years later, two more fellowships were planted on the west side of Melbourne; both fellowships worshiped at the same time but at opposite ends of the same community hall. One was an El Salvadorian Spanish-speaking congregation. The other was an English-speaking, second generation blended ex-Roman Catholic, Maltese, Italian, Yugoslavian group. The Sunday school, consisting of kids from both fellowships, met together in the center of the building.

One Sunday during the English-speaking service, a young man announced he had given his life to Christ that week. His baptism triggered seven more that Sunday, which became a lasting event in the life of the newly planted small church. The years following validated this young man's decision, as he continued in his walk with Christ.

Working with our small group of Christians in the remote frontier town of Kununurra in the Kimberley district, 3,000 kilometers (1,864 miles) northwest of Melbourne, had its challenges. Many of life's interesting characters have gravitated to this so-called "last frontier." Jan found work as a receptionist at the local hospital. Drunkenness among the local aboriginal population was a huge problem. I wondered how gentle little Jan would cope with blood-soaked bandages, fractured skulls, broken limbs, and drunken aboriginal combatants. I needn't have worried, she handled it well.

Financial and prayer support were provided by our home church in Melbourne and a wide group of friends. To further supplement our income in the Northwest, I was employed as a part-time quarantine checkpoint inspector on the West Australian/Northern Territory border. We were tasked with preventing the entrance of insect pests, plant diseases, and harmful weeds into the nearby Ord River irrigation scheme. My time there provided many interesting experiences, like seeing a man in the briefest of jocks making a beeline for a female staff member, who escaped screaming through the back door.

In another situation, we processed a truckload of 380 crocodiles. And still another resulted in the police intercepting a BMW carrying thousands of ecstasy tablets. There were certainly many unique situations, but the Lord also provided opportunities to witness, like my conversation with a man carrying a guitar. I told him, "When God gave out musical gifts, I was behind the door."

He sneered, "What gifts has God given you then?"

I replied, "He has given me a fulfilled life and an eternal destiny." Praise God for such opportunities!

The checkpoint staff was a colorful group and our church committed to praying for them. It is challenging to know whether you ever make any difference, but on the evening of my departure from the position, my boss said to me, "I don't know how it happened, but when you came, this place changed for the better." It was a God thing!

They gave us a farewell BBQ one balmy evening under a great big tropical moon that bathed the rugged Kimberley landscape with a soft golden glow. Some 30 staff were present; they said nice things and gave us lovely presents. It was a magical moment, but it was time to hit the road again. After three years and many adventures, the time was ripe for us to somber-heartedly return to Melbourne.

In 2000, the Lord led me to undertake an interim pastorate in New South Wales, and twice to serve as interim pastor in a remote mining town in West Australia before He prompted me to change my ministry to street evangelism in our multicultural city. In the course of that ministry, I handed out literature in many languages and testified to thousands of people. Some became Christians, some did not.

In the 18 years since my retirement, I have met some wonderful people. Recently I had the opportunity to pass on some acquired evangelism methodology to our current small church during a "Light the Fire" workshop on preparing testimonies. Approximately 30 folks attended, with promising results.

Men for Missions remains dear to my heart. I will continue sharing wherever God leads me to *Do, Go, and Give*, and will keep encouraging our local church. This aging 84-year-old has no plans for retirement. "And even when I am old and gray, O God, do not forsake me until I declare Your strength to this generation, Your power to all who are to come" (Psalm 71:18).

Regular Bible study and life experiences have contributed to my understanding of God's love through the crucifixion and His power through the resurrection. God's love, grace, and power, held in balance by the Lord Jesus and the Holy Spirit in accordance with the written Word, has become my mantra.

The Warren I Know

Mr. Justice James Turnbull
Ontario Superior Court of Justice

I first met Warren Hardig in 1989 in my law office. As soon as we settled in my office and began talking, I liked him. His broad smile, gentle voice, and engaging personality quickly captivated me. At that time, he had come to Hamilton, Ontario, Canada for an MFM Cabinet meeting. There he had learned that a group of eight in a men's discipleship group I was leading wanted to travel to Haiti.

He filled me in on the work of OMS and Men for Missions, and offered to travel to Haiti with us in August of that year. I was amazed he was prepared to do that for a group of guys he did not even know.

During that life-transforming week, all of us saw what a light Warren was in the world. He shared how God had touched him years before and led him to accept Jesus as his Lord and Savior. We were profoundly touched to hear how he had given up his job, as he and his wonderful wife Velma had committed their lives to full-time service to Christ working with Men for Missions. He encouraged us to go beyond our comfort zones and try to help with the ministry in Haiti.

Because of Warren's challenge, we created a charity called Joy and Hope of Haiti and have raised funds to build 27 schools, most of which are affiliated with pastors trained at the OMS seminary in Haiti. At the present, more than 6,000 children attend these schools where they learn to read and write as well discover Jesus and the hope

He can give to their lives. The executive director of Joy and Hope estimates that more than 125,000 children have attended schools built by the partnership of OMS and Joy and Hope. The seed for all this has been Warren's passion to serve Jesus Christ.

In my career as a lawyer and Superior Court judge, I have met many talented, generous, and wonderful people, and Warren Hardig is at the top of that list. He is one of the few people I know who has truly walked the talk; he has taken up his cross and sacrificed everything to serve Jesus. You've probably heard the question, "If you were arrested for being a Christian, would there be enough evidence to convict you?" The evidence is overwhelming that Warren is guilty. He has blessed a world of folks who have come across his path, which I remember every time I look at the beaming smiles of the children getting a Christian education in Haiti.

His friendship for over 30 years has been a great and inspirational blessing in my life.

An Extraordinarily Ordinary Man

Stanley Tam

Introduction by Warren Hardig

Stanley Tam has prayed with thousands of people to accept Christ in various settings. He is one of my heroes, and I would like to give you a deeper look into his heart.

Stanley is a giant of a man, a businessman who has spoken to multitudes of people in more than 30 countries around the world. He has given away his fortunes to various ministries that support the Lord's work. Many times, Stanley has been introduced with the opening line, "It is my privilege to introduce a man who needs no introduction," and they tell of all the countries where Stanley has served in ministry.

A few years ago, I flew into Dallas and boarded another flight to Houston. Seated beside me was Stanley, who was coming in from a different flight. What a delightful surprise! We shook hands and fastened our seatbelts. The cabin attendant offered us a beverage, and in just a few seconds, Stanley had shared the Gospel with her. Here was a man who speaks to thousands of people and yet will make every effort to lead a flight attendant to Christ in less than three minutes, with no microphone and no audience.

Stanley told me that at a family gathering on New Year's Eve, when everyone was retiring for the day, he decided to stay up to pray and see if there was anything God wanted to say to him. God told

Stanley, "You have money that doesn't belong to you." Stanley did some research and found he had an overage of about $5,000, so he sent out refund checks to several customers. Can you imagine being sent a check out of the blue from a company you do business with? That can make an incredible impression on people and let them know what your integrity is like, and surely sets you apart. Yet Stanley was only being obedient. God honored Stanley's honesty and blessed his business.

The customers would never have known about the overage, but Stanley Tam is the kind of man who seeks God's voice and responds with faith and integrity. He gave the refunds because in the quietness of the midnight hour, he resolved to obey God, even though it would cost him money. That's my hero, Stanley Tam.

On another personal note, while I was a regional director in southeastern Illinois, Men for Missions had a meeting featuring our first layman, Stanley Tam. We had the privilege of hosting Stanley in our home for the meeting. Our young son, Roger, about five years old, was sleeping by himself upstairs, and wanted to know if Uncle Stanley would tuck him in. Stanley went upstairs with Roger, tucked him in bed, and prayed a blessing over him. Roger thought Uncle Stanley was great, as did the rest of us.

At his current age of 107, Stanley still reads his Bible and prays more than four hours a day. He continues to reach out to anyone he meets to introduce them to the God who has been his constant companion.

That's my hero, Stanley Tam. I have asked him to share with you some of his story…

I was born in California in 1915, so I am 107 years old as of this writing. I don't know why the Lord has kept me around this long, but as long as He sees fit to give me breath, I will continue my daily disciplines of praying for four hours and spending another hour in the Word of God.

Before I had turned a year old, our family moved to Detroit for a few months and then settled in Lima, Ohio, where they had visited for a vacation and decided to stay. Dad and Mom bought a 170-acre farm where my two siblings, older sister Evelyn and younger sis Mildred, and I grew up. We helped harvest 2,000 bushels of potatoes and 1,000 bushels of beans each year. We also grew raspberries and strawberries, which I sold door to door in Lima.

My childhood was less than idyllic, with the home atmosphere frequently punctuated by quarreling and strife. My pride and joy was a pet pig I raised as a 4-H project, and many evenings I fled the cacophony in our farmhouse and quietly curled up with my four-legged friend for the night.

I attended McBeth School in Shawnee Township and graduated in a class of 50 students in 1933. For about a year I had a job with Montgomery Ward in Defiance, Ohio, working in the garage putting tires on customers' cars. I also received all truck shipments and signed the delivery slips. One time I signed for three shipments of furniture, but my boss said we had received only one, and he fired me on the spot.

Other than that incident, I was generally successful in my commercial ventures. I was the first young lad in our neighborhood to buy a Model T Ford, the first of three I would own over the years. Driving that prized possession bolstered my ego and expanded my business opportunities. I loved to cruise the roads, fully aware I was turning heads with my status symbol.

Hunger, From Beginning to Fulfillment

One of my childhood chores was milking the cows, usually after a long day of other labor. I had to round them up from the pasture and usher them into the barn. One night, when I was 10 years old, after dark had descended upon the farm, I walked the cows toward the barn.

I glanced up at the big, full moon rising in the clear sky and stopped in my tracks, transfixed by the beauty and wonder of the celestial theater. Like Adam and Moses and the Psalmist and countless others throughout the millennia, my thoughts turned to Someone out there. I instinctively whispered, "Who are you, God?" and followed that with a tentative commitment, "I would like to know You."

It barely classified as a prayer, but it was the first time I had vocalized any evidence of a spiritual hunger in my soul. I didn't overtly change my lifestyle for many years, but God heard that feeble petition and has worked in countless unseen ways in my life from that day forward.

God carved the path from me to Him through the living room of Mrs. Long. I worked as a traveling salesman for Zanol Products Company, which distributed household products, and stopped at her farmhouse. I gave my pitch and she agreed to purchase a couple items. Then she turned the tables on me and gave me a sales pitch I could not resist.

She started with, "You are a talented young man, but it does not matter how successful you become, you'll never be satisfied until you settle the most important of all questions in life – your relationship to God."

For two hours, she kindly and without intimidation answered my stammered questions and objections, and told me how Jesus had changed her life. The result of that conversation eventually led me to respond to an altar call at the church my cousin Bud and I attended.

That was when God answered my spiritual hunger pangs. Not only that, but He has allowed me to feast at His banquet table ever since. My full conversion experience is recorded in my book, *God Owns My Business*, on pages 12-19.*

Working With Dad and God

When I was fired from Montgomery Ward, Dad asked me to help him in his business. He received used x-rays from studios and medical laboratories and sold them for the silver content, which was extracted for recycled use. He asked me to be a driver, collecting film in 30 states. We collected about 13 tons of silver a year until they stopped using silver in x-ray film in 1958.

Dad switched to selling used plastic items and was doing $1 million in sales a year, much of the business being done in South America. He would spend time preaching in South America when he went there for business, and I eventually took over both the commercial and ministerial aspects of the business. It was mine to do with as I wished.

One time, in the middle of a sermon I was preaching in South America, I heard God tell me, "Stanley, I want the whole business." Three weeks later, I turned the entire multimillion-dollar enterprise over to Him. That turned out to be a great move, because now, even after I retired in 1990, the business does $77 million a year. I worked making furniture for several years because I enjoyed it, then I retired from all business ventures in 1998.

My business, Stanita Corporation, has donated $6 million a year to OMS, where I served on the board of directors for many years. OMS reaches 1.8 million souls every year, and I am honored to be a part of that.

Today, a large sign is posted on the headquarters building, "**CHRIST IS THE ANSWER**." That simple message has caused passersby to pull their cars into the lot and ask what those words mean, and we lead them to the Lord.

Warren with Stanley

My New Business

For the past 20-plus years, winning souls has been my main business. It is where my heart is.

I have preached three weekends a month in about 30 countries on six continents. My favorite nation is Korea, which I have visited six times. With 30 percent of the population being born again, it is, in my opinion, the most spiritual country in the world. Up to 150 people would come to the altar after a sermon, and sometimes every person in the congregation would step forward for prayer. I have also been to Japan four times and many other countries several times.

I don't start churches; I just get the people motivated to come in the church to get saved. I trust the Holy Spirit and He brings the people to the altar to receive Jesus as their Lord and Savior.

In 1938, I married Juanita, a pretty, born-again girl I met in Rockford, Illinois. For about three years, we traveled the United States in a trailer, preaching, praising the Lord, and selling products. Later, when the selling took too much time from our ministry and family life (we had four girls, two of whom have since passed on; the other two are 72 and 74 years old), we conducted all our business by mail.

During my decades in ministry, I have witnessed over 400,000 souls won to the Lord through meetings, sermons, altar calls, and one-on-one conversations. I praise God for the opportunity to serve Him and see these lives being committed to Him.

The Simplicity of Making the Sale

Many people want to know Jesus, but don't know how to meet Him.

I have found it is actually very simple to introduce them to Him. I just tell them how the Lord saved me and invite them in the same way to turn their lives over to Jesus Christ. It is that simple for anyone who wants to win souls. Tell others how your life has been changed by God, share how to receive Jesus (confess your sins and accept Jesus as your only Savior), and lead them through the sinner's prayer: "God, I know I'm a sinner. I want to turn away from that and turn toward You. Please forgive me of my sins and come into my life. I want to give myself to You and live for You. Will You please help Me? I ask this in Jesus' name, amen."

Fair warning: You'll have to give up some worldly pleasures to be fruitful in personal evangelism. I was born 15 years before the invention of television and a quarter century before the first commercial TV broadcast. I have always loathed television – and I still do. I consider it one of the "besetting weights" mentioned in the Bible. It steals time from Christians, when they could be serving the Lord instead of being distracted with silly programs. At worst, TV is a killer, destroying the sensitivity of the conscience and making sin look attractive. How many more souls could be won if Christians turned off the TV set and spent time in prayer, read their Bible, and witnessed to others about the loving Father and the saving grace of Jesus Christ?

Other Thoughts

In my book, *God Owns My Business*, I shared some thoughts that I think are useful to be excerpted here.

"It's good to have honest thoughts. The Bible tells us to prove all things, and to hold fast to that which is good." (p. 20)

"The genuine conversion experience involves an enormous vault from the finite to the infinite, during which time the convert remains essentially the same person he was before with one tremendous difference. Through the presence of the Holy Spirit, Christ begins a process of change. It's a wonderful, transforming experience. It begins in a moment and lasts for a lifetime." (p. 20)

"I'm convinced a lot of argument over the validity of the Scriptures would evaporate if people would come to the Bible in humility, realizing their need of divine light, recognizing the Bible as a lamp unto our feet and a light unto our path, and letting God convict and cleanse and motivate through His Word." (p. 22)

"I suspect God purposely made it difficult for the intellectual mind to accept the Bible as His inspired book. The miracles in the Bible have a disciplinary effect upon the quest for faith, compelling us to come to God in humble, childlike wonder, recognizing that He is God and that nothing is impossible for Him." (p. 22)

"The key to unlocking the inspiration held in the boundless reservoir of the Bible's pages is meditation. I ask God to make the meaning clear to me – not the theological or doctrinal meaning, but the relevance of this nugget of truth to my own life. What does it say in terms of guidance? Does it point out a weakness in my personality which needs to be corrected? Is it a window showing me the greatness of my Lord in a display of magnitude I have not seen before?" (p. 23)

"Remember that, whereas God often offers to work with us, His usual pattern is to work through us. He inspires our minds, guides our hands, directs our feet. 'I will instruct you and teach you in the way you should go; I will counsel you with My eye upon you' (Psalm 32:8). He instructs us and guides us, but the doing and the going is left to us. The requisite for this instruction and guidance is always to be clean and obedient to Him. When you seek to follow the Christlike life, you can expect God to check up on you, to test your motivations." (p. 65)

"To me, a Christian who has not laid up a store of Bible verses is like a hunter with a gun but no shells." (p.101)

"The five guideposts of my life:

1. Thank God for every adverse event.
2. I would rather hold a bolt of lightning in my hand than to speak against a brother.
3. Pay any price in order to be obedient to the Holy Spirit.
4. Administer in love and never govern in anger.
5. Pay three compliments every day." (p. 113)

"Soul-winning is the art of selling, raised to divine dimensions. Soul-winning is sheer adventure. No two experiences are ever the same. It's like being engulfed in the greatest of all dramas." (p. 137)

Leaving a Lasting Legacy

Warren Hardig

I live in a city that has a huge, modern football stadium with the sponsor's name on the roof and names of its famous football players on the inside around the second floor. We have at least two hospitals with family names in plain view for those who drive by. Streets and highways are named after politicians, coaches, and many others who made their mark on some page of history.

Recently I received a picture of some people who are making their marks on history in a vastly different way. They are part of the legacy of Gideon Schlecht, a godly farmer from North Dakota whose daughter and granddaughter have served as missionaries. In fact, the whole family has been or currently is serving the Lord in various capacities, unnoticed by much of the world. Gideon's son-in-law Don Smith has had an active role on the Men for Missions Global Cabinet. He has taken his whole family to Haiti to serve for an extended period of time. The picture shows Don with his daughter Mikaela Hultstrand and grandson Nieum.

Don Smith, daughter Mikaela Schlecht Hultstrand and grandson Nieum Hultstrand.

Leaving a lasting legacy is so much more than leaving an estate in a will or having a name on a building or plaque. Discipleship is more than memorizing Scripture. Both are good and should be a part of our lives. However, it is more important to live your life for Christ; pour into your family the witness that Christ gives strength, courage, wisdom, and hope for the daily challenges of life. Invest your finances in such a way that others might come to faith in Christ at home and around the world. Be a faithful, credible witness for Christ.

There is an interconnectedness with this picture of the Smith family. The Bibles for Cuba Project is the result of a second generation MFM man in Canada. Adolph Janke, one of the founders of MFM-Canada, lived his life in a manner that influenced his son, Marlowe, to be an MFMer and is now our National Director there. Canadian men and women are deeply involved with getting the Gospel into Cuba.

Back to the picture … Don Smith, Gideon's son-in-law, with his wife and family, is intent on spreading the Gospel every day. Don is holding a bank for donors to place cash in order to sponsor solar-powered fix-tuned radios to Radio 4VEH in Haiti. His daughter, Mikaela, is holding a second-generation bank featuring Sonny Solar, who promotes 4VEH as it continues to broadcast the Gospel. Nieum is learning about benevolence by making a glass jar into a bank where donors can place money to buy Bibles for Cuba. The Men for Missions network continues to leave a lasting legacy through their children, grandchildren, and great grandchildren.

Proverbs 20:7 states, "A righteous person who walks in his integrity – how blessed are his sons after him." And Psalm 71:17-18 reminds us, "God, you have taught me from my youth, and I still declare Your wondrous deeds. And even when I am old and gray, God, do not abandon me, until I declare Your strength to this generation, Your power to all who are to come."

May God find us ever faithful as we tell the next generation. Who knows what those who come behind us will do to make their mark on some page of history?

The Power of Agreement

John McLaughlin

Introduction by Warren Hardig

Henry David Thoreau said, "Most men live lives of quiet desperation." John McLaughlin perfectly exemplifies that an ordinary man sold out to Jesus lives a life of joy despite circumstances, has no fear of anything this world throws at him, and is not afraid to meet anybody's challenge since he knows God is with him. No life of quiet desperation here.

By being a part of the Broken Heart Club, my life has been and continues to be exciting, rewarding, and one of peace. It has been filled with things that make me weep and challenges too big for me to handle. Jesus has been dependable, and my prayer partners have helped me petition the Lord of Lords for help.

I am fortunate to be part of a large, worldwide prayer network. We, as an MFM staff, pray together often. I have a few men all across the world, from Scotland to Greenwood, that I can trust with anything. Velma and I are privileged to have our pictures on a lot of refrigerators and have dear friends who continually pray for us.

John, as one of my prayer partners, has walked with me through some of my biggest challenges. John has traveled with me in more countries than even Velma, partaken in several ministry opportunities with me, and has been my constant encourager. Today, the four of us,

John and his wife Karine, Velma, and I, are grateful for being together after praying a specific prayer that you will read about below. In his own words, here is John's side of the story …

My story would be very different if I had not learned that God has given us a mighty weapon against the forces of evil.

That weapon is prayer.

Sometimes God's answer is immediate and sometimes we wait. I was fortunate many years ago to find in Warren a brother in Christ; we developed a powerful bond and became prayer partners. Our first interaction was through Men for Missions (MFM). I trust Warren with my innermost thoughts, disappointments, and battles. As prayer partners, we have encouraged and strengthened each other through numerous adventures and trials. In all our battles, we have been like soldiers. Warren has had my back, asking God for a layer of protection from Satan.

I have claimed victories through many battles and circumstances because my weapon of choice was sharper than any two-edged sword. That two-edged weapon has been the Word of God, which came alive along with prayers of people from various parts of the world and prayers of my prayer partner. The Bible tells us there is power in agreement. "Jesus says, 'Again I say to you, that if two of you agree on earth about anything that they may ask, it shall be done for them by My Father who is in heaven. For where two or three have gathered together in My name, I am there in their midst' " (Matthew 18:19-20).

I can attest to that truth. One example is Operation Saturation, the vision to saturate Haiti with solar-powered radios – so Haitians could hear the Gospel on Radio 4VEH – and to build a new broadcast facility, since the old station was a dilapidated building.

How could men build a two-story, state-of-the-art broadcast center for Radio 4VEH without equipment or money? I will tell you how: men prayed in agreement. A tractor with a bucket was donated as our crane, and more than 20,500 volunteer hours were God-provided. Money poured in. Children gave their dimes to purchase solar-powered radios fixed tuned to 4VEH. God did the impossible.

When Warren and I agree in prayer, God listens and answers with protection, restoration, and deliverance. One of my long, difficult battles encompassed physical, financial, and emotional struggles. I suffered a business failure, lawsuits, and a devastating divorce. I had no income and the Internal Revenue Service (IRS) threatened to take my house, which was about all I had left. The battle and fire were so hot that I had little hope. How could I keep going? How could this be happening to a Christian? If I gave up, what impact would that have on my children and others? Those questions flooded me, and it would have been easier to give up.

It was through God's strength and the prayers of many, including my prayer partner Warren, that I was strengthened for the fight. It was a miracle of God when, instead of owing the IRS, they finished their audit and I received a sizable check from them.

God miraculously kept the door of our small manufacturing company open. During the 1980s farm depression, we dropped from 100 to 15 employees. The bank stopped short of foreclosing, but I couldn't take a paycheck. We were so poor our finance guy said the company couldn't afford to buy pencils. No one had heard of the garbage truck we started to manufacture, so no one wanted to buy a "no name" garbage truck.

Then the disheartening thought, *How could God use me again because of my failures, especially with a divorce?* My prayer partner encouraged me, prayed for me, and also got me involved with MFM in more ways than I had ever been before. Warren persistently prayed for the "no name" garbage truck company, New Way, to make lots of money and to glorify God. The "God Owns My Business" initiative* through MFM led me to dedicate our business to God, and to His glory it has thrived. The company became the largest privately owned garbage truck manufacturer in the country.

It has not been easy sailing; there have been events that would have closed the doors several times, but Warren and I kept praying. One time, the federal authorities came to lock the doors, but an employee convinced them they had the facts wrong (which they did). Another time, an investor demanded repayment of his more than $100,000 loan in one week and also demanded I leave so he could take over the struggling company. But God provided a stranger who loaned us funds without collateral. A fire started that could have destroyed the factory, stopping all manufacturing, but God intervened and we never totally lost production.

I have been able to share God's story in my life to encourage men in similar situations. We prayed for God to be glorified in such places as behind the Iron Curtain and in other communist countries. My faith increased when I was able to stand and praise God in Red Square, in Tiananmen Square, behind the Iron Curtain, in Haiti, and throughout other countries. In addition, I have been greatly encouraged by participating in Men for Missions, which provides the way for "ordinary men doing extraordinary things."

After hearing Bruce Wilkinson testify at a One Mission Society (OMS) conference about how the prayer of Jabez greatly expanded the borders of his ministry, Warren, Velma, and I were challenged to claim that Scripture, so we began to pray Jabez's prayer – and we still do today. Jabez felt inadequate and wanted to do more for God, so he prayed, "'Oh, that You would bless me indeed and enlarge my border, and that Your hand might be with me, and that You would keep me from harm that it may not pain me!' And God granted him what he requested" (1 Chronicles 4:10).

When Warren, Velma, and I started praying the prayer of Jabez, we drew a circle and targeted numerous prayer requests, which included a wife for me, an affordable home for Warren and Velma, and, during a critical time for MFM, 70 qualified men to bless MFM and expand its borders. Velma persistently added a twist, a woman perfect for me. And after 17 years of being single, God miraculously answered that prayer with Karine, the woman who met everything on my "impossible" list. I, in turn, met everything on hers. God answered Warren and Velma's prayer for a comfortable home suitable for hospitality close to OMS, within their budget. And He continues to expand the borders of MFM by connecting men globally to reach the world for Christ.

God has answered prayers of protection for Warren and me on many MFM trips. Our team prayed before a trip and each night as we traveled in the war-torn country of Burundi, Central Africa. One night, as I lay under my mosquito tent, I heard small arms and mortar fire. Since I was in a cement block building and near the floor, I just hunkered down. Warren slept through it all. There had been a rebel attack just one-half mile away.

Military troops blocked the roads for some time but then lifted the blockades so we could travel to Gitega. We were stopped at numerous military checkpoints and saw many machine gun nests on the hillsides guarding the road. We were aware of the dangers, knowing that rebels had killed people making this same journey.

God had prepared hearts when Warren gave his testimony at a small church packed with villagers, and the Holy Spirit moved people to respond in prayer to follow Jesus. A week or so after we left, 200 villagers were killed by the rebels. Some of those people we met may be in heaven. We are thankful this trip was covered with prayer. God protected.

Another time at a crowded train station in Moscow, I was about 10 feet away from Warren when I saw a band of tough-looking people surrounding him. Eight gypsies attacked Warren, grabbing for valuables. Warren was loaded with cash we were delivering on behalf of our ministry. Velma immediately swung into action with her purse, yelling, "You can't have him! You can't have him! He is mine!"

They fled. Why would the gypsies give up so quickly unless the Lord of hosts scared them away? God answered the prayers of our team again that morning.

God poured blessings into our lives during a trip to Tibet. After a prayer walk through the Dalai Lama's palace and seeing tens of thousands of Buddha statues, I prayed "Jesus" while monks were chanting.

Karine and I had spent the evening with our New Way dealer and some customers. Early the next morning, I was awakened with a sharp, intense pain in my chest. I prayed to Jesus, but the pain continued. I knew I had to go to the hospital. My wife immediately asked for prayer via a quick e-mail. Unbeknownst to me, Warren, my family, and many in MFM were praying, and God answered in overwhelming ways.

We went to the empty lobby. A man walked in and took us to the Lhasa hospital. Our employee, Michael Jin, interpreted the unique situation to the medical staff and managed the pay-as-you-go system for drugs and a bed in a cold room. After several tests with limited results, my wife said, "We need to get out of here."

I didn't want to be stuck there and die, so in dire pain I rode an hour to the airport.

Our daughter Natalie, back in the U.S., found us a flight to Chengdu, as God had foretold us of an American doctor there. After more tests ruled out a heart attack, the doctor insisted we travel as soon as possible to a more advanced hospital. I didn't think I could make it, but God provided. The first flight available that night was a red-eye to Beijing and a recommended Western-style hospital. The Chengdu doctor called the ER doctor in Beijing, where God had placed a Christian American ER doctor. By the time we got there, God helped him recall what he had read about a perforated esophagus. A few more tests confirmed the diagnosis.

We didn't think about how to pay for all this care. The hospital asked for $50,000 up front, but accepted Blue Cross Blue Shield, my insurance. My experienced surgical doctor and nurses provided excellent education and care for 23 days. Our son, John, called one of his USA doctors and found out he had studied with my Beijing surgeon. They discussed my case and gave my family updates. Daughters Natalie and Kim were soon *en route* to encourage my recovery and exercise as I walked with poles and feeding bags in the hospital hallways and stairs.

The time came when I was ready to go home. But how? God provided. Our son Mike found an insurance clause so the cost of my flight nurse back to Iowa was covered instead of us having to mortgage our home. Soon I was healed enough to taste mashed potatoes and eat ice cream and dance with my wife! Experiencing how our Mighty God could do ALL these things built a giant step in growing our faith and trust in Him. The prayers of agreement were answered (see Matthew 18:19).

Velma also experienced a critical medical emergency a few years ago. Prayers were prayed immediately for an aortal dissection surgery that had a less than five percent survival rate. God spared her life not once, but twice because a year after her first emergency surgery, a longer, more complicated surgery to prevent another dissection was required. The throne room of God was boldly approached in prayer by Warren and me as well as others, and God provided an expert surgical team. He answers prayers. We give Him the glory!

Over time, God restored in my life many things the locust had eaten and the thief had stolen (see Joel 2:25; Job 42:10). "The thief comes only to steal and kill and destroy; I came that they may have life, and have it abundantly" (John 10:10). Warren and I have learned to pray in agreement, with clean hearts, no doubts, with the expectation that God is answering. He has answered prayers for ministry, business, family, health, and the ministry of MFM. Although we've had victories, we still pray for many needs and difficulties. There is greater power in joining together. "Again I say to you, that if two of you agree on earth about anything that they may ask, it shall be done for them by My Father who is in heaven. For where two or three have gathered together in My name, I am there in their midst" (Matthew 18:19-20).

I believe all of us need someone we can pray with who can strengthen us, encourage us, and agree with us as we pray for God's will in our life. I agree with Dr. Wesley Duewel, former OMS president, who said, "Prayer is always the pathway to miracles."

Now that I think about it, I'm a walking testament to that.

**"God Owns My Business" initiative is described in the Glossary.*

Elaine

Warren Hardig

Elaine's story may seem out of place in a book about laymen, yet "There is neither Jew nor Greek, there is neither slave nor free man, there is neither male nor female; for you are all one in Christ Jesus" (Galatians 3:28).
Velma and I had a part in Elaine's coming to faith in Christ. God's display of His sovereignty in allowing us to reconnect and be encouraged by His presence in Elaine's life is miraculous, like the parting of the Red Sea.
Perhaps not as noteworthy, but a miracle nonetheless.

A Personal Word from Warren about Elaine†

When we present opportunities to go on MFM ministry teams, someone inevitably asks, "Wouldn't it be better to just send our money?" After answering that question, I was once asked, "So, what are you doing for the drug addicts right here in Detroit?"

Nor is it unusual to run into other prejudices such as, "Why go to Russia?" or "The Asian people who've come to America are taking our jobs!" or, about converts, "After all your efforts, will they remain faithful followers of Christ?"

So, is it worth ministering in nations other than our homeland? If our hearts are pure and our motives are right, yes – a thousand times, yes!

---

†*Some personal and/or church names have been changed for their protection.*

God is so wise and so holy. "All the paths of the Lord are lovingkindness and truth to those who keep His covenant and His testimonies" (Psalm 25:10).

When I pray for Elaine, I wonder, *How does God know which Elaine I am praying for in China's 1.4 billion people?* I don't know that answer, but I do believe He hears, He is helping Elaine, and He is all about helping us worship Him. Elaine's story is included herein to address the questions of the religious.

God's Sovereignty Through the Years and Across the Miles

I have had the incredible privilege of traveling around the world, participating in different ministries, seeing some amazing sights, and hearing the incredible sounds of life. But the true wonder of the world is the joy of seeing people come to Christ. There are bumps and scrapes, and lots of bleeding along the way; yet at the end of the day, we revel in the excitement of experiencing redemption come to people, whether they are from southern Illinois, China, Russia, or South America.

One of the greatest stories of my life began in October 2001, though it had a shaky beginning. A month after the attacks on the U.S. on the morning of 9/11, we took a team to China for almost three weeks. To alleviate the concerns of friends and family, our team of 24 compiled an extensive e-mail list of those who would pray for us daily. Each day we sent back comments from team members and informed the prayer warriors where we would be the next day (seeing the Great Wall, the Terra Cotta Warriors, Tiananmen Square, etc.). We were led by two great missionaries, Lowell and Rod Williamson, a father and son team who just couldn't be beat for their care, servant hearts, and love for people.

Team member Maury Graham wrote about one day's activities:

> *We had an inspiring experience today, listening to the wife of an 88-year-old pastor. Her husband had graduated from the OMS seminary in the late 1920s, before the communist occupation.*
>
> *In 1958, he was imprisoned for his faith and spent 21 years and eight months in confinement. Most of that time was spent in the far northeast, close to the Soviet border, where winter temperatures routinely dipped to 30 or 40 degrees below zero.*
>
> *They worked nine hours a day at manual labor, without adequate nourishment. Despite all the hardships, his faith never wavered. And when he was released in December 1979, he resumed preaching, even though he was on (government) probation for 10 years.*
>
> *We were emotionally moved to hear of his faith, and it increased our resolve to do what we could to help the church in China increase its evangelistic outreach.*

Our tour guides offered wonderful hospitality. Each region had an expert on hand to help us understand where we were.

Elaine, our national tour guide, grew up in Shanghai. As a young lady, she loved dancing and the arts and attended the Foreign Language Institute. She said, "I actually did not have much choice, as my math was so poor!"

After graduation, Elaine married and had a daughter. When we met in the Beijing airport, we saw her as a bright, beautiful woman, just barely out of school. She looked so young, it was hard for us to believe she had a 10-year-old daughter.

I have gone to China several times. Since 2001, we have taken people to four or five major cities in China to show them how God is doing special things. There are many opinions and all kinds of statistical data about China. The geographical layout and population militate against numbers that can be agreed upon. Our guide Elaine was with us the whole time we were in China, and the whole team (a fun group of 13 from the United States and 11 from Canada) fell in love with her. The people were zealous in their beliefs, and God was at work. Many in the group talked daily to Elaine about their beliefs.

Our first Sunday in Beijing, she took us to a church regulated by the government. You hear all kinds of stories about churches in China, and they may be true … somewhere in the country. People have differing opinions about the Asian churches, but our impressions were positive because of the people we met there. The message, however, was flat and empty since the pastors at these churches were not allowed to talk about salvation, forgiveness, or the lordship of Jesus Christ.

In the last city before we visited Hong Kong, we went to Pastor Samuel Lamb's house church. He was about 90 years old and a high-profile Christian. During his presentation, he slammed his hand down and said, "Persecution is good. Through persecution our churches grow. My church was at 500 people and now we are at 1,500."

Pastor Lamb's three-story church was about 15 feet wide and 30 feet long, and 500 people crowded into the church area. The latecomers sat on little four-legged pie pan type stools. Pastor Lamb talked to us about what he was doing and how his church was growing. He said he preached the same message four times a week so everyone could hear the Gospel. He broadcast his sermons via closed circuit TV on the first two floors and lived on the third floor. Elaine accompanied us, and she heard his preaching that explained the Gospel, salvation, and worship.

That evening after church, we visited a mall. Elaine took Velma back in a secluded corner and asked, "What do I do about all this information I have been given about Christianity?"

Velma advised her to deeply consider it to be true and to ask God to give her discernment and understanding. They spoke of many other things, including that Elaine and her husband were arguing.

The next day, Elaine took us to the train station to depart for Hong Kong. All the travelers thanked her profusely for being such a good tour guide. Velma was the last one to get on the train. She and Elaine hugged each other and talked for just a few moments. Velma encouraged her once again.

Elaine whispered in Velma's ear, "Thank you. I now know the difference between the two churches and what you've been trying to tell me. I understand." Elaine had experienced worship in a government-regulated church and a true Christian church. One gave us what the government expected, following many rules and regulations, while the other had taught the true and living Gospel message.

We rode across the border to Hong Kong. After arriving, we got our luggage and boarded the bus to be greeted by our missionaries. They said, "Welcome to Hong Kong. We should pray for Elaine immediately because before you got out of town, the police were at her office to interrogate her about why she went to the house church with you."

We prayed for Elaine – and are thankful for the wisdom God gave her. She asked the police, "What's the difference? I went to church in this city; I went to church in that city and another. What's the difference? A church is a church, isn't it?"

They didn't really have the answer, and God protected her. She had to give our names to the police, so we didn't go back to that city for a couple of years; in fact, we only recently returned there. We prayed for Elaine and found out from the Williamsons that on New Year's Eve 2001 her boss, a Christian who had set up our travel, led her to Christ.

When we visited China the following autumn we wondered, "Will we see Elaine? Maybe she will be our tour guide again." But we didn't get Elaine; instead, a delightful young man did a good job for us. We still wondered, though, *Would we ever see Elaine again?*

China has many three-, four-, and five-star hotels, along with lots of buses filled with European, Australian, and American tourists. They have tourism down to a science. The restaurant tables are filled promptly from one hour to the next, and in three minutes' time, a group from another country will replace the previous group. It's the same way with the buses. They have buses going to the Great Wall, the Pearl Factory, the Silk Factory, and they click you right through.

Once, as we were going out to get on the bus (though I don't recall which city we were in), Velma heard, "Velma! Velma!" She turned around – and there was Elaine. We each hugged her and heard briefly about her faith and how she was doing.

She asked joyfully, "Did you hear what happened to me?" We assured her that we had heard of her conversion and had been praying for her.

Elaine continued, "It is so wonderful, I want to tell everybody, but I can't."

We were struck by the contrast. Here was a woman who wants to tell everybody about Jesus, but can't; in America we can, but we don't.

We had a few moments together, and we thanked the Lord for that. At that time there were 1.3 billion people in China, and we got to see one woman, our friend Elaine. We were amazed!

We took another group to China in 2004 and went to see the Terra Cotta Warriors in a theater with a 360-degree screen that shows the history and legend of the warriors. That day, we lunched at the large hotel on the Terra Cotta site, and I heard my name called. I turned and it was Elaine! I got up, ran through the aisle and hugged her, and as soon as Velma saw her, she came running, too. We had just a few precious moments of fellowship with Elaine. Again, we found that her faith was strong and she was doing well. Her daughter was growing and her husband was good. Then we took off and didn't see her again.

I still stand amazed that out of 1.3 or 1.4 billion people, we would again run into Elaine.

Two years later, we went back to China with quite a diverse, interesting group of educators and accomplished musicians and had a great time together. On the last Saturday of the trip, we traveled on the Lee River and stayed in a beautiful resort. On Sunday morning, we had a church service at the resort in an all-glass room. Lowell and Naomi Williamson, outstanding musicians and vocalists, led the worship. Three people on the team gave testimonies: Mike McIntosh from Canada, Marge Pauszek from Indiana, and Michael Jin, an Asian businessman. Doug Carr from Australia gave the message.

Our Muslim tour guide told us later, "I've never attended anything like that." She enjoyed it, then shared with us about her life. We never know when God will allow us ministry opportunities.

After the church service we went to eat breakfast on the resort's deck, which offered a beautiful view of the mountains. Martha, one of the team members, took her food outside to eat on the deck, which had a small step she did not see. She fell hard, and everything went flying through the air – food, dishes, and chairs. I immediately began a 911 to God for His help. "God, how am I going to get her moved from here? Please touch her, help her," I begged. Velma was there immediately to help Martha and keep her stable until we could determine the extent of her injuries.

A doctor from another tour group and a nearby lady came over to help Velma. The lady got in the mix and was scurrying around in an attempt to help. Velma thought, *If you would move over, I could do this a little better.* They determined that Martha only had a bruised lip and no broken bones. As we were getting her in a chair, the lady turned her face up to Velma and said, "Velma? It's Elaine." So we saw Elaine again for the fourth time, in another city and hundreds of miles from previous encounters.

We hugged her and Velma asked, "Elaine, how is your faith?"

"My faith is strong, my faith is good," she answered.

"How is your marriage?"

"Our marriage is wonderful. We are not arguing anymore." We asked about her daughter, who also was doing well. We had 10 minutes of intimate fellowship with her and then she was gone. She had to take her tour group to its next stop.

What brings me great joy is people like Elaine who appear out of nowhere in a country of over 1.4 billion people. We've seen this woman four times in four different cities and, except for the first time, never for more than 10 or 15 minutes at a time.

After we returned home, Martha wrote in a note to Velma, "I've been sharing my testimony with Methodists, I've been speaking to Nazarenes, I've been speaking at Wesleyan churches. God is awesome!" She is having the time of her life raising money for China.

Martha's life was changed because she went to China. Although she fell and could have had broken many bones, she has nothing but praise and is talking with people in her home state of Kentucky about the Lord and her changed life. Martha found her life-changing journey, living in the joy of being a contagious, world-missions oriented Christian.

We are not only witnesses in other countries, we witness here as well. The local church is the hope of the world. That's more than a good thing to say, it is the absolute truth. I've had the privilege to be in churches in the Democratic Republic of the Congo, in Newton, Illinois and in Medellín, Colombia, and I have seen that the local church really *is* the hope of the world.

The only thing we have to give away is the abundance and overflow of Jesus Christ in our lives. We are not about a self-improvement program; we are ambassadors of Christ, united in building God's Kingdom, committed to reaching the multitudes by touching individual lives. We've had a good time with Him and we are ready to again go for Him. And who knows? Maybe we'll see Elaine along the way!

Praying at Home and Around the World

Gene Bertolet

Introduction by Warren Hardig

My first meaningful friendship with the Bertolet family was with Gene's parents, who were affectionately called Pastor Earl and Edna. I always appreciated the warmth of their Peoria home and the kindness they showed to me when I visited.

In November 1969, Velma and I were invited to a Men for Missions dinner in Albion, Illinois. Next to each place setting was a magazine titled *ACTION,* the official publication of Men for Missions International. I found out that *ACTION* was the handiwork of Gene Bertolet, a young, talented, successful graphic artist, and the son of Earl and Edna. Gene had been an employee of a major manufacturer and inventor in Indianapolis. The owner once commented that Gene's patent drawing and drafting skills were among the best he had ever seen.

In obedience to God, Gene left the business world and joined what is now One Mission Society. Gene's drawing board became his pulpit as he helped spread the Gospel through countless pieces of literature for OMS and MFM, proclaiming God's message to the multitudes in many countries. Gene is a strong, Bible-believing Christian with a keen sense of purpose. He often says, "I don't want to reach a ripe old age and look back on life with regret, realizing I'd missed it."

Gene's personal walk with the Lord, guided by being marinated in God's Word, has by the guidance of the Holy Spirit enabled him to lead several individuals into a personal relationship with Jesus Christ. Gene dedicated more than 50 years of outstanding ministry to OMS and MFM. Even now as he has stepped back from his graphic design role, he continues to pray for the nations of the world, and he is attentive to any hungry heart needing spiritual help.

As a veteran of the U.S. Army, other veterans and I have a true appreciation for the Prayer Warfare Manuals that Gene has designed and feel strongly that we should focus on strongholds of evil in our praying to defeat the enemy of our souls.

Gene is a very capable spiritual leader who, like former OMS president Dr. Wesley Duewel, prays at a deep level of intercession. Both men saw and understood intercession to be the life-and-death matter that it is. Prayer is a matter of life or eternal damnation to those drawn to the Lord. Gene's vision for the lost is vital. He says it best: "You focus on the harvest, not on the combine."

Gene's life is so intertwined with MFM and follows so much history of it that I asked him to expand what he shared. So in his own words, here is his story …

A Good Foundation

I was born Robert Gene Bertolet on June 26, 1935, in Irving, Illinois. For some reason I was always called by my middle name, Gene. I was the first of six children and shortly after my birth, my family moved to Peoria, Illinois, where Dad worked on several government-sponsored construction projects for the Civilian Conservation Corps (CCC) following the Great Depression. He eventually found employment with Caterpillar Tractor Company, where he worked for the next 35 years. Mom was a stay-at-home, full-time mother. She never learned to drive a car and was always home as we children were growing up, coming home from school, and leaving the nest to make our way in the world.

Dad and Mom were not overtly religious. Dad's background, I believe, was Lutheran, and Mom's, Methodist. We did not attend church as a family, though my parents didn't object to neighbors taking us to Sunday school, church, and special church programs like evangelistic meetings, Christmas and Easter services, and Vacation Bible School (VBS). So, I was exposed at a very early age to Bible stories, flannel-graphs*, and what I thought was the "truth" that the good go to heaven and the naughty go to hell.

From about age six, I feared not being good enough. About age 12, I began a more serious consideration of what I was hearing about the Bible and God. Among our family, friends, and neighbors were varied confusing, unconvincing, and fanatical voices – charismatics, astrologers, fiery preachers, and hypocrites. But at age 19, something clicked in my innermost being. The path to personal peace with God became clearer to me as the concepts of the Bible became increasingly interconnected and understandable.

Times were tough in the post-Great Depression era. We were poor by today's standards, but we didn't really know it because everybody we associated with was also poor. Family life was generally good and predictable with routine radio programs, chores, scheduled activities, and meals with plenty of food to satisfy a big family. Chicken dinners were interesting. Before the chicken shed burned down, Mom could go to the chicken pen, catch one, wring its head off, dip it in boiling water, pluck the feathers, cut it up and fry it, with no refrigeration needed. I can still see Mom heading for the shed, emerging with a chicken, wringing off its head (jumping up and down flatfooted like she was turning a crank), and then flinging it in the yard to flop. After the shed fire, the chickens ran wild in a pen overgrown with tall weeds. Dad had to go hunting in the back-lot jungle with his trusty .22 to bring a chicken home for dinner.

Very early in childhood, I became aware of God and an undefined sense of accountability. As early as six or seven years of age, I was drawn to God. I remember being taken to Bethany Missionary Church by a schoolteacher who lived across the street. One experience of those early days is etched in my memory. The scene was VBS in a dank basement classroom of the local Church of God. In my mind, I can still see the sagging curtains on the basement windows, the peeling paint on the stucco walls, a flannel-graph of a Bible story on a rickety easel, and can still taste the warm orange Kool-Aid and stale cookies.

Perhaps another reason that particular VBS experience is unforgettable is the furor it raised at home. A teacher was expounding on the gross sins for children to avoid – smoking, drinking, dancing, movies, etc. I raised my hand and said, "My dad drinks lots of beer." At that young age, to me, two or three beers a week seemed like a lot. Soon the good ladies of the church had Dad branded as the town drunk and the focus of prayer meetings. Dad was furious at me and them. But it was ultimately a tender and informative time, as I was at least exposed to the concepts of sin, salvation, the Bible, and prayer.

I remember experimenting with prayer around that time. We were experiencing a severe drought and farmers were losing crops and the well was beginning to go dry. I got on my knees at bedtime and begged God for rain. That night we had a terrible thunder and lightning storm, resulting in flooded fields, downed trees, flattened cornstalks in the fields, impassable muddy dirt roads, and power outages. I was *sure* I had caused the mess and was fearful others would find out.

Later, at about age 12, I began to seriously think about God, the Bible, prayer, good versus bad, heaven and hell. I wanted to know for sure how to make peace with God and avoid the consequences of not doing so. Because of my failures in school and Dad's harsh reaction, I wondered if smart was good and dumb was bad. I remember asking Mom if I had to get smart for God to like me. She assured me that He accepted me just the way I was, though He surely wouldn't mind if I did better in school.

Much later in life I would understand more fully the theological, doctrinal, and especially spiritual implications of my search. But it seemed at that time each church or supposed authority on the subject had differing views. All, however, seemed to agree that certain words (*being saved, born again, changed life*) and a commitment to God, preferably spoken at a church altar, and a subsequent act of baptism, preferably by immersion, were all necessary. Consequently, my spiritual quest continued at the altars and through the baptistries of the Church of God, Bethany Missionary Church, and a Baptist church. Yet the questions still haunted me: *Had I said all the right words? Done all the right things? Was I good enough to gain heaven and avoid hell?*

I have purposely not said much about my grade school and high school experiences, partly because school for me was generally not a pleasant experience. During my school years, life seemed to be on three separate tracks. Home life was a refuge from the apparent failures of school life, school life was a diversion from the tense and chaotic home life, and an emerging spiritual life was creating obligations to do better at home and school, but I seemed to lack the power to change either. Thus, none of the tracks were fun or fulfilling. It seemed I was always behind in class work, which annoyed teachers. Behind in classwork meant I was also behind in homework, which upset Dad.

Differences with Dad

Much later in life, Mom confided in me what might have been the missing piece in my deteriorating relationship with Dad. She told me that Dad's expectation for me, even at birth, was to someday attend West Point. A Civil War buff, he saw military strategies and victories as ultimate achievements. But it became evident early on that I would never qualify for an appointment to West Point.

Maybe it was his disappointment that amplified his reaction to my many academic and athletic shortcomings, or maybe not. We never discussed the matter because I wasn't supposed to know about it. However, because chaos at home and tension with Dad were growing, in the late fall of 1952, I moved out of the house and in with a school friend and his dad. It saddened all, especially Mom. Since I had no intention of going to college, I just wanted to take the easiest route to put school behind me, graduate, get a job and a car, and begin a life of independence.

I moved back home before graduation in May 1953, though I spent as little time there as possible. Dad got me a job at Caterpillar, starting in the mailroom and later in the drafting department as a parts catalog illustrator. But trying to live at home while enjoying some degree of independence was frustrating.

One day, perhaps in a moment of exasperation, Dad said, "Maybe you ought to join the Army and learn some discipline."

So, on a rebellious impulse and youthful whim, I took his advice and volunteered for the draft at an Army recruiting office. Almost immediately I was sent to basic training at Fort Leonard Wood, Missouri. Mom was not supportive of Dad's suggestion or my reaction to it.

Army Days

Without a doubt the Army experience became the best part of my life up to that point. The discipline of highly structured Army life had both positive and negative results. On the one hand, the military took complete responsibility for food, lodging, exercise, clothing, equipment, and combat training. On the other hand, unquestioning obedience to authority and doing only what was commanded seemed to stifle individual initiative and creativity, which is precisely what was intended.

Initially I needed the discipline and security of superiors. Later it became clear to me that even within the well-disciplined military unit, I was ultimately responsible for my personal safety, security, and spiritual well-being.

Perhaps I was thinking about that spiritual well-being aspect one day about a week into basic training. I remember coming into the barracks after a particularly hard day of training. Exhausted and probably a little discouraged, I sat on my bunk to rest. Nearby was my Bible I had brought from home. Impulsively, or maybe guided by an unseen hand, I unzipped the cover and opened it. Obviously, I hadn't opened it until then or I would have found what was tucked in the pages. Mom had placed a $10 bill and a handwritten letter in the Bible:

Feb. 17, 1954

Dear Gene,

I am writing this the day before you leave. I hope you find it soon, by putting it in your Bible maybe you will find it when you need it most. You know Gene, daddy and I both love you very much but I could never show my affection for you kids, when you got older by words and kisses, but only when you were little and daddy is the same way. We've always wanted the best for you and maybe we expected too much of you. Anyway I'm so sorry things haven't gone smoother for all of us, it seems people always hurt the ones they love the most. Try to be a good boy and a good soldier. I hope with all my heart that all the best comes to you from this life.

Lots of Love, Mom

Pvt. R. Gene Bertolet

After the completion of eight weeks of basic training at Fort Leonard Wood, I had 30 days of furlough. My lifelong connection with Caterpillar Tractor Company, as Dad's and my former employer, influenced my application to the Army's Tractor Scraper School. I was accepted, so I returned to familiar surroundings, but to a different unit. I completed the eight weeks of Tractor Scraper School without any embarrassing incidents, though there were many close calls. My orders, along with those of several buddies, were for Okinawa, the southernmost island in the Japanese chain. Sometime during the two-week voyage from Seattle to Okinawa my reassignment orders were changed, as were the orders of the other guys I had trained with in Tractor Scraper School. Our unit was no longer designated "Heavy Equipment Operators." Suddenly we were Military Police (MPs).

We newbies looked good in MP garb – white hats, white gloves, blue scarves and lanyards, MP arm bands, polished black nightsticks, and .45 pistols. I felt uncomfortable and awkward, wondering how I would react to the first real-life challenge, but things in my past came to the rescue. My art history and drafting experience qualified me to be assigned to MP headquarters, producing posters, organizational charts, a variety of maps, and a monthly newsletter. My only real MP assignment in full uniform was driving a jeep as the Duty Officer's chauffeur and armed bodyguard.

At last I was free of parental authority, except for Mom's haunting words in the letter she had placed in my Bible, "Try to be a good boy and a good soldier," and Dad's exhortation, "Join the Army and learn some discipline."

To be a good boy in this environment would indeed require discipline. Other voices from the past, pastors and teachers, warned that sinful choices and actions have eternal consequences. But conversations in the barracks revolved around the vilest of topics and activities. Driving the MP Duty Officer put me at the scenes of horrific crimes and their aftermath, glaring reminders of the consequences of grossly sinful actions and undisciplined lives.

Seeking God in the War Zone

In those chaotic surroundings in Okinawa, I began to search for some sort of spiritual connection. Structured religious activities in the military revolved around the post's chaplains of the various faiths presenting "character guidance" chats and grainy black and white movies. I sometimes attended Sunday Protestant services at the post chapel, which were rich with oratory but short on practical application. Sunday evening services, however, were led by a solid Baptist chaplain, Captain George Park, whose sermons were Bible-based with applications aimed at moral discipline.

After only two months in Okinawa and with little spiritual support, I felt like I was at the edge of an evil, corrupt whirlpool. To step away from it meant lonely isolation and commitment to a disciplined lifestyle that I probably could not endure alone. To step in meant exercising less and less restraint and riding the tide of debauchery down the drain. I really wanted to "be a good boy and be a good soldier," as Mom had written, even though that meant swimming against an overwhelming tide.

At that stage of my life and Christian experience, I could draw only on what I had heard and seen among the professing believers I had encountered at evangelistic meetings, churches, and school. My personal experience with God apparently consisted of faith in what others said about God, words I had said, and rituals I had participated in to be "saved."

But that experience was being severely tested in the crucible of secular military life set against the backdrop of the pagan Asian culture. If there was a spiritual experience beyond what I had encountered that would enable me to live above the emotional and cultural fray, I was ready to embrace it. I was feeling lost and in need of a strong, encouraging friend to keep me on the right path. I was, in fact, reaching out for a personal connection with God.

There were a couple of guys in the MP barracks who seemed to be riding above the moral chaos. One of the fellows didn't drink, smoke, or swear. In fact, he didn't even drink tea or coffee. He was a Seventh Day Adventist. The other fellow, O'Roark, was a burly, hairy guy from New York. His accent was hard to understand at first, but he had a peaceful resolve about his life and a faith that impressed me, and I wanted to know what kept him on the straight and narrow path.

He invited me to go with him to a Saturday evening Gospel meeting at the Kadena Airbase chapel. The G.I. Gospel Hour meetings were sponsored by Youth for Christ, an organization I was familiar with. Their work in Okinawa was to evangelize and disciple military personnel. The following Saturday O'Roark and I went to the small Quonset chapel at Kadena Airbase.

Moment of Decision

The moment I walked into the Quonset on Saturday, November 13, 1954, I felt at home. The group gathered inside, numbering 50 or so, was comprised of men and women in civilian clothes. There was no way to distinguish between the branches of the military, officers from noncommissioned personnel, or visitors from regulars. The format of the service was predictable and typical of a Youth for Christ meeting – a few choruses, a meet-and-greet time, announcements, and introduction of the speaker, Rev. Bob Shelton, a missionary from Formosa (Taiwan), serving with Overseas Crusades (OC).

I really don't recall what he said. All I vividly remember is being on my knees at the altar saying words I had said many times before: that I was a sinner and desperately in need of a Savior. But there was something strangely different that Saturday evening. Something like an electric switch clicked inside, and I was suddenly connected to a source of power that could overcome the environment that was trying to draw me in. All things suddenly became new. "Therefore if anyone is in Christ, he is a new creature; the old things passed away; behold, new things have come" (2 Corinthians 5:17).

After the Saturday evening meeting, I was introduced to a Navigator missionary, Bob Boardman, who, with his wife Jean, were new on the island. "New" is not the right word. As a Marine, Bob had stormed ashore years before in the notorious bloody battle for Okinawa. Wounded in the throat by Japanese gunfire, he spoke in breathy tones, barely above a whisper. He had recently returned to Okinawa as a missionary with an incredible love for the Japanese people and a desire to minister to us military people, whose struggles he knew well.

Dick Hillis' Overseas Crusades had just formalized an agreement with the Navigators, which enabled the Navs to administer follow-up and discipleship mentoring to OC contacts. Bob's discipleship group met Tuesday evenings in the Boardman's humble Japanese-style hut in Naha. For nearly 27 months, I received rich, undiluted discipleship training, learning how to study and memorize Scripture, how to share my faith, and how to mentor another disciple in the spirit of 2 Timothy 2:2: "And the things that you have heard from me among many witnesses, commit these to faithful men who will be able to teach others also."

Unlike the shaky spiritual quest of my early youth, I knew for certain Jesus Christ was my personal Savior. God had forgiven my past rebellion toward Him and my parents, and I was on the right path toward solid spiritual maturity and heaven. I passed through the waters of baptism one last time when Chaplain George Park baptized me at Yaka Beach, Okinawa, in the Pacific Ocean, December 11, 1955.

In March 1956, a spiritual life retreat was conducted at the Yaka Beach Center, probably jointly hosted by G.I. Gospel Hour and the

Navigators. Bob Boardman was there as facilitator. My faith had grown dramatically under Bob's Tuesday evening teaching and through my personal time in God's Word. The Navigator training model then involved progressive teaching about the Word, Prayer, Obedience, and Witnessing. I was in the Word, memorizing the 108 verses of the Nav's *Topical Memory System**. I was beginning to experience what God was saying through the Bible as words spoken by Him as a person; He was speaking to me. With that sense of His presence, I began to view prayer as actually speaking to a person who was actually listening.

Counting the Cost

An incredible world event occurred Sunday, January 8, 1956. Five missionaries were martyred in Ecuador by Auca Indians. Jim Elliot, Nate Saint, Ed McCully, Peter Fleming, and Roger Youderian were attacked and speared by a group of Huaorani warriors. Bob shared the tragedy with our group the following Tuesday evening; he was a personal friend with some of the martyrs.

The time together that evening was a teachable moment. We discussed the high cost of discipleship and whether the cost is really worth it. Mark 8:34-37 took on new meaning: "Whoever desires to come after Me, let him deny himself, and take up his cross, and follow Me. For whoever desires to save his life will lose it, but whoever loses his life for My sake and the Gospel's will save it. For what will it profit a man if he gains the whole world, and loses his own soul? Or what will a man give in exchange for his soul?"

Something clicked inside, and for the first time I knew I was meant for missionary service in some capacity, someday, somewhere.

"You and Your Household ..."

Another significant event at the Yaka Beach Center was almost too profound to put into words, but I will try. At the retreat, I had a growing sense that the past hostile relationship I had with Dad and Mom had to be faced and somehow resolved. I was overwhelmed with both remorse for my actions and my love for them.

On Sunday, the final day of the retreat, many guys had already departed to return to their outfits. Sometime before midnight I asked a couple of the fellows if they would join me on the beach to pray for my parents, and for my relationship with them. We knelt together on the beach and prayed. Sunday before midnight on Okinawa was sometime before 10:00 a.m. Sunday morning in Peoria, Illinois.

I returned to the barracks Monday and wrote a seven-page letter to Dad and Mom, expressing my regrets for the past and presenting a complete outline of the plan of salvation, with Scriptures spelled out. I dropped it in the mail. A letter in those days took a week to be delivered and another week to get a reply, so I didn't expect a reply to that letter for about two weeks.

One week later I received a letter from Mom, which could not have been a reply to my letter to them. I could hardly believe what I was reading.

She said that Sunday morning (the same Sunday we were praying on the beach just before midnight) they got up and Dad announced they were going to church. As providence would have it, they went to Bethany Missionary Church, where an evangelist was beginning a series of meetings. According to the pastor, barely before the invitation was given, Dad ran from the back of the church and fell across the altar, pleading, "Help me, help me!"

The pastor said in all his years of ministry he had never seen anything like that. That evening they went to the special services at Bethany and Mom went forward to accept Christ as her Savior.

The exact time of our intercession on Okinawa synchronized perfectly with Dad's moment of salvation in East Peoria – and God's timing in heaven. A week later I got another letter from Mom, which began, "I guess you know by now that your prayers were answered."

Dad and Mom both began their Christian walk as active servants and teachers in Bethany Missionary Church, and they later became actively involved in overseas missionary projects.

Decisions at the Crossroads

I don't recall much about departing Okinawa in late January or early February 1957. I do remember that the troop ship was bigger, nicer, and faster than the converted freighter which had taken me and 1,500 other men to the island in 1954. It was only about a week until we sailed under the Golden Gate Bridge and docked in San Francisco harbor. The Red Cross warmly greeted us, thanked us for our service, gave us doughnuts and coffee, then hustled us onto waiting buses. We were then separated according to destinations – some for our next military assignment and others for discharge.

My next assignment was Fort Sheridan in Chicago, where I was honorably discharged from the Army on February 12, 1957, six days shy of three years of military service. I was grateful to have survived the potential pitfalls of Army life, proud to have served my country, glad to once again be on American soil, and happy to be headed home.

Job hunting after the Army was interesting. On one hand came the temptation to seek a career position with Caterpillar that offered benefits and retirement. On the other hand, I had the G.I. Bill benefit that would pay for four years of college. As far as I knew, no one in our family had ever graduated from college. Could I be the first? I tried several jobs: selling cutlery, installing telephones, driving a de-tasseling tractor for a group of Bethany kids trying to earn some summer income, and working as a rubber cutter (hand layout and cutting of rubber plates for offset printing). But in retrospect I can say quite honestly that nothing seemed to satisfy as a career choice because God apparently destined me to a higher purpose, and He was narrowing my choice to Bible college.

The desire to go to a Bible college was certainly strong. The decision to actually try to go was quite another matter. It would not be easy. Preliminary inquiries at Fort Wayne Bible College (the college of the Missionary Church) indicated that my high school grade transcript made acceptance for enrollment impossible. However, the pastor at Bethany Missionary Church, the Rev. Ralph Ringenberg, had connections at FWBC. He wrote a personal letter on my behalf, stating that I had been in the Army, had the funds through the G.I. Bill, and had somewhat matured, but most importantly, had sensed a call to Christian ministry. He asked that the college grant me an opportunity to enroll. FWBC responded they would grant me one semester of probation, and I would have to maintain at least a "C" grade average to continue.

I wanted to see hope and promise in the offer, but my old nature could only see disappointment, failure, and the fulfillment of Dad's prediction that I would probably quit or get married and drop out of school. I was facing a major life-changing decision, and I think I was expecting some supernatural guidance. But I saw no vision or dream, heard no voice saying, "This is the way, walk in it." So, I considered not even starting college and returning to Caterpillar for a career commitment.

I have a precious memory of Mom and me sitting on the steps of the front porch in the cool night air discussing the options of going or not going to Fort Wayne the next day. The incredible journey of the next 60 years, which are now history, literally hung on my decision that night. At her urging I decided to make the journey, and a truly new and exciting life began. Perhaps God was whispering His direction through her that night.

I was 23 when I stepped onto the campus of FWBC, at least four years older than most of those entering the freshman class. I suppose the expectation was that since I was older, I was probably wiser. Other students my age were married and living off campus, or were pursuing additional credits toward higher degrees. But I was carrying the baggage of four wasted years of high school. After all, I hadn't planned on going to college, but there I was. Of course, I wanted to succeed academically and earn a degree.

For me the Bible had become the most important body of truth and knowledge in the universe, and I wanted to master its message and application. I was hoping God would be impressed with that noble motive and be obliged to grant some degree of success. I would need all the help and encouragement available. Financially, the G.I. Bill of Rights allocation of $110 per month (the same amount I was paid while on active duty) for college was sufficient to underwrite tuition, room, and board. Nobody but Uncle Sam would lose out if I bombed in college. I was grateful that others, especially family and church people, were not financially vested in me or my FWBC venture. Obviously, I did not have high hopes of making it through the first semester of probation, much less completing eight semesters of a four-year program. But I did survive probation with a little better than a "C" average.

The first floor of the south wing of Schultz Hall, the boys' dorm, was the living quarters of the Dean of Men, the Rev. Harold W. Ranes, and his family. His wife, Betty, was an unofficial dorm mom, giving a listening ear to typical concerns and complaints of young men who were many miles away from home for the first time. She also folded and stored the dorm laundry and household supplies. Although I was not in need of a surrogate mom, I enjoyed occasional conversations with her in the supply/laundry area on the third floor of the dorm. Their teenage son, Tim, was a frequent visitor in our dorm room.

Boy Meets Girl

In the fall of 1959, at the beginning of my second year at FWBC, Tim visited our room. He said his sister, Juanita, from Indianapolis was going to visit the family for a brief stay, and he wanted me to meet her. She visited, we met and chatted, and she returned to Indianapolis.

Considering the distance between us, I gave little thought to any future contact. But I'll have to admit I was certainly not opposed to spending more time with the attractive, sweet, petite brunette from Indianapolis whenever she visited her family. A couple of weeks later she returned to campus for a visit and a date seemed to be in order, so I took her with me to a speaking assignment at the Fort Wayne Rescue Mission on skid row. She held up quite well as I led her down the center aisle past a couple dozen disheveled guys to a front row seat. I wondered if she would ever agree to go on another date with me.

I'll probably never know what really transpired in the Ranes' wing of the dorm, but Tim announced that Juanita was moving from Indianapolis into their Schultz Hall apartment. She was going to start work as a secretary for a local commercial kitchen supplier. I think the family was expecting me to immediately take up the pursuit, but a relationship with the daughter of the Dean of Men seemed a bit ostentatious and perhaps not fair to her or the family. I was, after all, a struggling academic with a less than stellar upbringing who quite possibly would not make it through three more years of college. As a preacher's daughter, I figured she deserved better – perhaps a bright, aspiring pastoral studies student, destined for the ministry or a professorship and a lifestyle more familiar to her.

Yet, as our dating got more serious and personal, I knew Juanita and I were meant to be together. We talked about marriage, even though I was scarcely halfway through college. Echoes of Dad saying, "You'll probably quit or get married and drop out" resonated in my thoughts. Juanita was willing to accept my proposal but cautioned that tradition required I get her dad's permission.

That was a tough one. Who was I really addressing in that dim-lit office adjacent to the Ranes' quarters? Juanita's dad? The Rev. Harold W. Ranes? The FWBC Dean of Men? My *Old Testament Survey and Poetical Books* professor?

And how did he view me? A questionable student who recently survived academic probation? A guy with no well-defined career objectives, no financial security, and certainly no promised future inheritance?

Well, the meeting went about as suspected. He asked, "What can you offer my daughter?"

I said, "Right now, I have a part-time job at Sears."

He said, "That isn't much."

He then said, "You know she has special needs."

I asked, "Like what?"

He said, "She has a very narrow foot and needs special, expensive shoes." He added, "She has been hurt (referring to the tragic loss of her fiancé in an automobile accident) and will need much tender understanding."

I promised to be as understanding and gentle as possible, even though that might mean sharing Juanita with her ghostly memories for a time. Perhaps he was just filling his role as a protective father, but he finally gave me permission to marry his beloved daughter.

In the late fall of 1959, I purchased a diamond engagement and wedding ring set at the Sears jewelry counter. As we dined at a Chinese restaurant, I showed her the engagement ring and asked her to marry me … and she said "Yes." It was a memorable evening indeed. Maybe it was the excitement of the moment or more likely the shrimp-in-cream-sauce dinner, but we both then got terribly ill. We struggled back to the dorm; I left her in her folks' care and went to my room to recuperate, which we both quickly did.

We were together most evenings, as our schedules permitted. Her mom got to know me better than perhaps she intended, as my prankster instincts drifted to the surface. One afternoon she had invited Juanita and me to coffee and cookies, served up with all the pomp of an English tea, with an assortment of antique porcelain cups, saucers, and the works. I was not an accomplished coffee drinker (only with lots of cream and sugar in those days), and sort of lacked the social graces required by the occasion.

Juanita's mom, wanting to give the conversation some general direction, commented, "I suppose you noticed these china cups and saucers."

I knew they were antiques, valuable, and no doubt special heirlooms, but said, "Oh, you don't need to apologize, Mrs. Ranes, nothing ever matched at our house either."

The moment was priceless. She was speechless but soon realized that her future son-in-law was going to be a fun challenge.

The winter months passed quickly because of study for second year first semester finals and preparation for second semester. We were also anticipating our wedding in early June, between my second and third year of college. It was time to settle on a degree major, and I chose Bachelor of Science in Missions. Since that day in 1956 when Bob Boardman shared the story of five heroic missionaries martyred in Ecuador, missions had tugged at my heart. I wanted my life to matter, and I sensed there was no higher calling than missionary involvement. Juanita and I had discussed the possibility of living in a mud hut in the jungles of Africa. She seemed okay with the hypothetical, but I wondered whether reality might pose a challenge for us, should we be led into that environment.

Life Together

Juanita and I were married June 4, 1960, at Emmanuel Baptist Church, where we had attended and were served by the Rev. Harold Ranes, her dad, who officially directed the traditional ceremony. After a brief honeymoon in Florida, we returned to a small off-campus apartment and settled into a routine schedule, balancing married life, work, school, and tight finances for the next two years. In the fall of 1961 as I was preparing for my final year at FWBC, we discovered we were going to be parents. The following spring, in the midst of final exams, David entered our lives, a joy to be sure, and dramatically altering our familiar routine schedule.

I graduated from FWBC May 22, 1962, with a double major in Bible and Missions. It was a time of special celebration. My parents got to meet David, their newest grandson, when they attended my graduation. I'm sure Dad was proud, especially when it was noted in the program I was graduating "with honor." Admittedly, I felt satisfaction in graduating and finishing well, despite Dad's predictions, which probably subconsciously drove me to excel. As nearly as I can determine, I was the first in our family line to graduate from college. But that accomplishment pales in comparison to those in our lineage who followed.

Because my college major and career interests were missions oriented, I felt the obvious next step was to consider job opportunities in the Missionary Church. But the doors to service in areas I felt qualified for seemed closed. However, Juanita's brother-in-law, Howard Young, a sales manager for a lock company in Indianapolis, was aware I had drafting experience from Caterpillar and said the lock company had an opening in their drafting department. It wasn't missions, but at least it was a job, even if temporary.

With the move to Indianapolis, the choice for a church home was obvious. Most of Juanita's relatives attended Hope Church, a vibrant and rather affluent congregation of about 800 with an annual mission's budget of almost $100,000. Juanita and I were quickly merged into the Young Married Class, consisting of couples in their late twenties and thirties. David, who was still an infant, fit nicely into the nursery program where Juanita and I often participated.

Church worship in the '60s and '70s was very traditional — choir, hymns, organ, preaching, midweek prayer meetings, and a variety of social events. As we continued to attend, however, it became clear that not all was right with the church or its pastor, who was facing allegations of improprieties. My enthusiasm for church and spiritual values began to wane. I knew there was much more to the Christian life than I was experiencing, and I began to prayerfully seek it. Ironically, the eroding spiritual environment of the church played an important role in God's clear guidance for our future ministry.

The job at the lock company soon began to sour. The president and founder of the company almost immediately drafted me from the engineering department to be his personal designer/draftsman. He was an avid and eccentric inventor as well, and had applied for many patents. He was especially pleased with my unique ability to produce highly technical patent drawings, a skill I mastered doing illustrations for the Caterpillar parts catalogs. He once commented that I was among the best he had seen (though his son was actually much better). Some of his contraptions and patent applications were, to me, a waste of effort and money. Also, with our expanding family and a new home, I needed more income.

Late in 1963, I was contacted by a smooth-talking "headhunter" (a person hired by corporations to fill positions for clients). He said I was a good fit for a drafting/mechanical engineering position at an instrument company in Speedway, Indiana. So, I gave my two-week notice to the lock company; we moved to Carmel, Indiana, and I went to work designing mechanical components for graphic recording instruments.

Time Waits for No One

In the early days of February 1964, when I was just 29, we were eagerly awaiting the arrival of our second child, a daughter we would name Pamela. Apparently my "midlife crisis" came a bit early, and that summer and fall I grew restless. I felt a keen awareness I was on the verge of casting the die for the rest of my life. I wrestled with the reality that one day I would reach old age, and I feared I would look back over my life with regret.

Decisions had to be made, and I sensed I had a very short window of opportunity. The reality was that almost everything in my world had seemingly lost value and purpose. The one exception, fortunately, was Juanita and the children. Although the choices concerning the future were mine alone to make, there was love in our home.

Underlying all other considerations was the painful realization that I was missing the spiritual perspective and purpose that once motivated my decisions. Was I to seek a God-ordained ministry, or was I to continue on the path of secular employment? If the latter, could I trust God to ordain for me (us) a ministry in that secular environment? I felt a sense of urgency, though no one around me was aware of my personal turmoil. I was waiting for God to act in dramatic fashion to point the way. I see in retrospect, though, He was actually waiting for me to take the first purposeful step in a new direction.

In the spring of 1966 Hope Church held a missions event and two participants, Burt and Bernardine Biddulph, represented the Oriental Missionary Society (OMS), headquartered in Greenwood, Indiana, a suburb just south of Indianapolis. Their daughter, Judy Finn, was in our Sunday school class. At a meet-and-greet session following an evening meeting, my conversation with Burt got very interesting, very quickly. He asked what I did for a living. I told him I was a draftsman and commercial artist.

"That's interesting," he said, "OMS is in the process of moving our headquarters from Los Angeles to Greenwood and our staff artist is not making the move. Are you willing to consider assisting with some pressing needs until we find a local source?"

I agreed, and a day or two later I got a call from Eleanor Burr, editor of OMS publications, who wanted to meet me. OMS Vice

President Bill Gillam and Eleanor made the journey from Greenwood to Carmel, and we shared a cordial visit. OMS's pressing need was a brochure to promote their annual missions convention, to be held at Winona Lake in June. I agreed to do the design and artwork for printing. At the time, I thought OMS could possibly be a good client for my fledgling advertising business.

Working With, Then For, OMS

I was impressed with the vision and mission of OMS and the people I came in contact with in the course of doing business. Working with Eleanor Burr, I produced the artwork for *ACTION* magazine, a publication of Men for Missions, the laymen's ministry of OMS. I wanted to know more about the organization, and was increasingly interested in plying my artistic skills to help meet their needs. It was clear to me that if I committed to doing all the work they needed, it would be a full-time job.

To do all their work as a contracted source would be financially prohibitive for OMS. Another possibility was to sell our new home, resign from a new well-paying job, and move to Greenwood. Strangely, that option seemed reasonable and appealing. Juanita reluctantly agreed, and we began the application process in February 1966. By July we were approved and moved to the Greenwood headquarters office.

In February 1967, Juanita and I joined Harry and Eleanor Burr and a team on a "crusade" (now called "ministry team") to Haiti. For many on the crusade, the Haitian poverty and squalor were a shock to the senses. To me it wasn't much different from what I had experienced for nearly three years in Okinawa.

There was one characteristic, however, that was uniquely and strikingly different – voodoo worship. It went far beyond the traditional Buddhism in Asia. Animal sacrifices and rituals were intended as worship of the devil. Later I discovered that voodoo witch doctors had dedicated Haiti to Satan in a blood covenant in exchange for his help in defeating their French oppressors. As one Haitian told me, "Haiti may be 25 percent Christian, but it is also 100 percent voodoo." In other words, voodoo has such a grip on Haiti that it permeates every aspect of Haitian culture, even the church. Before that trip to Haiti, I had never personally witnessed demon possession and exorcism. All of this became relevant decades later when I was thrust into the middle of Haiti's spiritual warfare and the battle with spiritual darkness.

A Year to Remember

For me, 1968 was an incredible year, a year that marked the beginning of several spiritual ventures. That summer we visited Juanita's sister, Jackie, and her family in Houston, Texas. Jackie's husband, Howard Young, was the regional sales representative for the lock company. His sales region was large and included all of Texas and parts of adjoining states. I rode with him on a sales trip to west Texas. On the long trip back to Houston, he told me about his newfound love of God's Word, the Bible. By then he had read it through several times at the rate of 15 chapters a day.

I was impressed. There I was, a missionary, Bible college and Navigator graduate and Sunday school teacher, and I had never read the Bible completely through from Genesis to Revelation. On that trip, I determined to read the Bible through at least once a year, and I have continued to do it for the past 50-plus years. I began to experience true faith in a Person, not in the words on a page.

The more I knew about God, the more I wanted to know, and that inspired my desire to pray more often and more deeply. I had discovered a faith that was straining to act, driven to do something for and with God. That's probably what James had in mind when he penned "faith without works is dead" (James 2:17). Later, I discovered the Bible's word for that experience is "abiding" (John 15:5). The next two decades marked the zenith of my professional, missionary, and spiritual life. There were, of course, later periods of God's obvious guidance and blessing, but nothing quite like the '70s and '80s.

Just as Howard's influence in 1968 changed the course of my spiritual walk, I think my nudging was possibly a turning point for Howard. Obviously, I didn't know at the time where Howard and his family were headed in relation to God's plan for them. I assumed that, as a successful lock salesman, his calling was probably to generously support missionaries and missions, hopefully through OMS and MFM. With that in mind, I told Howard I was leading part of a team to Haiti early in 1969, and I invited him to join me and to be prepared to play his trumpet, do a little speaking, maybe even some preaching. He did not warm to the idea. He was "too busy" and it was "probably not the best use of his time or money."

"Tell you what, Howard," I finally said, "you go and if you don't think the trip was worth it, I'll personally refund your money."

So Howard went with me on that 1969 Haiti crusade.

About dusk, we landed in the stifling heat of Port-au-Prince and were immediately bused to a church service. The place was packed. Two or three bare light bulbs hung from the ceiling, and people were peering through every window and door opening. We were ushered to the front and seated on the platform. The latrine was just off the dirt platform where we were seated, and I thought the stench, the tropical heat, and the press of humanity might signal a rough start to our few days in Haiti. Then the service began with Haitians singing and worshiping. Less than two hours in Haiti and little more than 10 minutes into a Haitian worship service, Howard leaned toward me and said, "I won't be wanting the money back."

Howard took his boys on a Haiti crusade a few months later and sent Jackie on yet another such adventure. Harry Burr, the executive director of MFM, seeing Howard's leadership potential, encouraged him to prayerfully consider leaving the business world and becoming part of MFM as National Director. Howard and his family were ready, and in 1971 they moved from Houston to Greenwood.

Saturation in the Word

I began reading the Bible through at the rate of about 15 chapters a day, completing each reading through in about three months. Later, I settled on about five chapters a day, six days a week, completing each trek in little less than a year. The earlier reading plan was five chapters in the morning, five at noon, and five in the evening, six days a week. I was probably on my third or fourth time through and was reading five chapters in the book of Acts in my OMS office during lunch. I came to Acts 1:8: "But you will receive power when the Holy Spirit has come upon you; and you shall be My witnesses both in Jerusalem, and in all Judea and Samaria, and even to the remotest part of the earth."

I had memorized that verse years before as part of the Navigator Topical Memory System. It was analyzed at Bible College in the study of the book of Acts and my studies as a Missions major. Yet in that particular reading it seemed unfamiliar and strange, like I had never seen it before. What was happening?

I closed the door of my office and knelt beside my desk, asking God to help me understand the strangeness of the hour. It dawned on me that I was not seeing those words as part of Scripture, but they were coming to me as a personal promise.

At that time, I had never personally led another person to Jesus Christ. Could the promise be literal or figurative in the sense that my ministry would impact world missions? Through the years as a Christian, I had accumulated guilt for not being an effective witness who won souls. Suddenly the guilt was gone. I was free to serve God as I was, where I was, without preconceived expectations of what spiritual success should look like. I had the promise that He would make me part of His plan for reaching the uttermost parts of the world in His own good time.

Claiming Territory for God

Immediately after my encounter with Acts 1:8, I had the desire to claim my Jerusalem (Greenwood) for Christ. But how? I considered driving the streets while praying for the families related to the homes. That proved to be too impersonal. It occurred to me that virtually every home had a telephone (keep in mind this was in 1969), and the phone numbers were listed in a Greenwood phone directory with names in alphabetical order – a ready-made prayer list. There were approximately 10,000 names, each representing a family. My rationale was that if I prayed for everyone represented through the Greenwood phone book, I would most likely not meet or witness to anyone I hadn't prayed for.

One morning in a staff prayer time I heard Charlie Spicer praying for Greenwood in phrases that resonated with my own emerging prayers for the community. I shared my phone book strategy with him. I was still in the As and Bs and Charlie said he would begin with the Zs and work backward. Our praying was simple: that every name, and the household related to it, would discover a vital connection to Jesus; that believers would be encouraged and share their faith; and that unbelievers would be moved by the Holy Spirit to seek peace with God through Jesus Christ. Interestingly, Charlie began to reap a harvest in the Greenwood community, many from my half of the vineyard, but we rejoiced together.

Meeting Warren

About that time, I was invited to speak at an MFM retreat at Turkey Run State Park in western Indiana. The date was February 14, 1970. I'm certain of this because whoever scheduled the meeting had failed to note it was Valentine's Day, not the best time for a gathering of guys to be together for a weekend without their wives or sweethearts. I had agreed to be on the program, speaking about the importance and consistency of being in the Word. Following me on the program was Stanley Tam, a dynamic lay speaker and soul winner. I really felt like "filler" in the program, sandwiched between the inspiring music of blind bass player, Chuck Merrill, and the renowned Stanley Tam.

As the music time ended and I was set to speak, two businessmen from Olney, Illinois, Warren Hardig and Ken Milone, entered the meeting. Warren was a fertilizer salesman and Ken was a supervisor at a bicycle manufacturing company. They had just returned from an MFM crusade to Haiti and were overflowing with excitement, eager to report on their mission experience, so my time was (gratefully) shortened.

I told of my introduction to the Word through Howard, how reading through it over and over was making the words personal, as if being spoken to me by a Person. I shared the Acts 1:8 experience and my desire to pray for Greenwood as my Jerusalem, using the phone book as a prayer list. Referring to Charlie as a prayer partner for Greenwood who was introducing locals to Christ, and aware that Stanley the soul winner was next on the program, I awkwardly concluded my session with something like, "If God's promise in Acts 1:8 means I'm only to influence the world through prayer and support the ministry of others, I'm okay with that."

I wasn't convinced anyone was at all interested or motivated to get into the Word. I retreated to the back of the room after the session and stood next to Chuck Merrill. He knew me by my voice, and I recall that he spoke a reassuring comment. Stanley began his session by handing out a short syllabus and said, "If you're in a dark area you may want to move to where there is more light."

Chuck leaned toward me and whispered, "Am I in a dark area?" There was something about the levity of the moment that relaxed me from the anxiety of the previous hour. Chuck was a wonderful friend and I miss him.

Miracles at a Home Bible Study

On the return trip from Turkey Run, Jim Miles commented that he was moved by my remarks and had made a commitment to begin reading through the Bible. Then he made an interesting proposal. He said we needed to start a home Bible study; he would get it organized and I could teach. The offer was timely. I was saturated with the Word from consistent reading through the Bible and ready to share. Teaching the study group was a mixed blessing, with times of joy and tears.

Those Thursday evening meetings were often punctuated with profound demonstrations of answered prayer. A local Mexican contractor and Vietnam veteran came, claiming, "I've been to Bible studies all over the world and I'm curious about what you're teaching." A few days later I introduced him to Christ. A few days after that, his wife called and said, "Something has happened to him. Whatever he's got, I want it too!"

A Colombian immigrant came to a meeting; the Mexican interpreted, and before the evening was done, he led him to Christ. A huge, muscular woman, a Black Panther from the inner city of Indianapolis, came to a meeting. Soon, Jim Miles was leading her to Christ. Likewise, a barefoot, shirtless hippie in coveralls from a local college came and Jim introduced him to Christ. We had been in earnest prayer for the angry, threatening husband of a lady in the group. One evening he showed up unannounced. We didn't know what to expect until he blurted out, "Okay, I give up! How do I climb the fence or raise the shade to get God off my back?"

There were many more precious and memorable evenings, too many to recount here. In many ways I was serving as the pastor to a small congregation. It was an incredible 24/7 opportunity and obligation, but during those 18 years our family life, personal ministries and work at OMS and Men for Missions also continued. The Bible study group was considered by many to be only a sideline to my primary ministry obligations with OMS and MFM. However, I embraced it as a rich and fulfilling ministry opportunity.

The Harvest Continues

In the days following the Turkey Run Retreat, the floodgates of opportunity opened. An insurance salesman trusted Christ as Savior in our living room. A few days later a mail machine repairman wandered into the mission office during the noon hour. As he waited in my office, he too, trusted Christ.

Paul Totten

Later that month, March 30, 1970, to be precise, Paul Totten, a highly decorated former WWII POW, real estate broker, and community leader came into my office. I had met him in 1966 when we worked together on a Greenwood Chamber of Commerce brochure. He wanted some advice on a newspaper ad he was putting together. The ad featured a listing of his accomplishments: Greenwood Man of the Year, multi-million-dollar real estate salesman, chairman of this, president of that, etc. I commented that it was an impressive list and asked if there was anything else.

He said, “How about dedicated Christian?”

I asked, “What does that really mean, Paul?”

He said he had been a lifelong member of his church, serving on every commission at least once, and on most commissions twice. He said he was generous with his giving and time, and always tried to live by the Golden Rule.

Without thinking, I heard myself asking, “Paul, has all of that brought you peace?”

Incredibly, Paul hung his head and tears filled his eyes.

I invited, “Paul, do you want to meet Jesus, the Prince of Peace?” He said that’s what he needed, so that’s what we did.

That morning when I had walked into my office, I had the strange sense there would be just such an encounter. I was prayerful and expectant throughout the morning. I presumed anyone in my office would be seated in the only other chair, so I tucked a Four Spiritual Laws tract between some books at the edge of my desk near that chair. At the noon hour, I remained in my office, thinking there would perhaps be an encounter like that with the mail machine repairman.

When the call from Paul came, I didn't make the connection. In fact, I hadn't considered him a candidate for conversion. His sterling reputation in Greenwood convinced virtually everyone that whatever Christianity was, he had it. So, my agreement to spend some time on his project was a courtesy I hoped wouldn't interfere with the anticipated encounter of the day. But as Paul entered my office and took a seat in that chair next to those books and the pre-positioned tract, I sensed, "That's the man, and this is the time."

From that moment on, as in previous encounters, I became an observer, not really in control of the dialogue. There was, however, a calm assurance that the encounter would spiritually impact Paul's life. And it did. He matured and gave exceptional spiritual leadership to Greenwood's Christian Businessmen's Committee (CBMC).

That was only the beginning of an incredible adventure with God as the literal fulfillment of Acts 1:8 began to manifest. The amazing thing from my perspective was that I felt like an observer to unfolding events. Every day was a new adventure, filled with anticipation. I began to see people and situations as divine appointments.

One memorable event was visiting with my sister in Pekin, Illinois. It was evident that the conversation was evolving into one of those appointments. I was merely a spectator of the Spirit at work in her heart as she tearfully surrendered to Jesus.

I wondered if all that was happening was a direct result of my commitment to the Word and prayer for Greenwood and beyond. I believe that was indeed the case. What I had learned in theory in Navigator training in Okinawa was beginning to produce a harvest of believers in Greenwood and beyond.

Expanding Horizons

In 1971, the next phase of that Acts 1:8 promise began to unfold. My spiritual horizon was expanding from my Jerusalem (Greenwood) to my Judea and Samaria (surrounding towns, counties, states).

As word of the people coming to Christ in Greenwood leaked out, I had invitations to speak about it in various MFM and church venues. I was amazed how little success qualified one as an "experienced soul winner" in Christian circles. The fact, however, is that more than 95 percent of professing Christians never personally lead another person to Christ.

I could identify with that reality. It frustrated me for years, especially as a Navigator trained to do that very thing. Public speaking was never easy or natural for me and it was even more difficult in that context. I was obligated to share my exciting experiences of leading others to Christ without focusing on the techniques that resulted in that success. Because of the decision in 1968 to read through the Word of God over and over, I had discovered real faith and trust in the person of Jesus. That living faith quite naturally resulted in effective prayer for others. So to me, soul winning was a result of spiritual discipline, not necessarily an activity to be taught and mastered.

Together Again

It was a *déjà vu* experience for me as Howard's family moved onto the OMS campus in 1971 and he took up responsibilities as MFM National Director. We were together again in similar roles we had enjoyed at the lock company. In those roles we were often in meetings discussing the design and engineering aspects of products the sales department deemed necessary. Now we were in meetings discussing the printed materials MFM deemed appropriate to promote the work of MFM and OMS in the homeland.

Howard's leadership style took many off guard. He was direct, willing, and quite able to make decisions and assume full responsibility for his actions – a stark contrast to the usual consensus mentality that routinely condemned projects to death by committee. Howard's vision for MFM was to establish and maintain at least 100 councils (groups of men who regularly met to discuss, support, and pray for missionaries and MFM projects and needs) across the U.S. and Canada, which was not all that different from his responsibility at the lock company, overseeing the activity of regional representatives across the U.S. and Canada.

Family Changes

As David and Pam moved from pre-school to kindergarten and on to primary school, we began to experience "empty nest syndrome." For a number of reasons, we considered the adoption alternative to add one more child to our family and that journey presented its own set of challenges. At a school board meeting, Dr. Bob, another member of the Christian school board, asked me how the adoption process was going, and I gave him the less-than-promising update. He asked if we would be interested in adopting a baby at birth. He and a colleague worked with expectant mothers who chose to put their babies up for adoption. We were certainly interested and were already pre-qualified as adoptive parents.

Dr. Bob said there was a young mother expected to deliver in early January 1972. Our entire family went before a judge to clarify our intentions to adopt, and then in a second court appearance, actually adopted the child before he or she was born. That meant we would be regarded as the birth parents on the birth certificate and assume possession at the hospital. So, we waited and waited.

On New Year's Eve, December 31, 1971, we asked a dear friend and OMS colleague to sit with David and Pam while we went out for the evening to celebrate with Harry and Eleanor Burr. We told the sitter of the possibility that we might get a call from a doctor friend. When we arrived home after midnight there was a note that the baby was born, but no other details. The next morning, New Year's Day, it was difficult to get information, but we finally learned we were the parents of a healthy boy. We finally got the official approval that all the details were covered; we would take delivery of our newborn son, Daniel, on January 3, 1972.

The Gene Bertolet family, circa 1972.
Danny, David, Juanita, Gene, Pamela.

Korean Connection

Also in 1972, an OMS missionary in Korea requested a brochure to raise $10,000 to produce Sunday school training materials for 2,000 OMS churches ministering to 500,000 believers. As I analyzed the request and tried to formulate wording that would explain the impact of donations on the future of the church, it was obvious to me that $10,000 would pay only for an initial printing of materials in Korea. There would need to be recurring solicitations to keep resupplying the need. It occurred to me what was needed were levels of graded Sunday school materials that could be used and then reused by the next generation of students. So, I proposed translating a set of graded English Sunday school quarterlies, incorporating Korean cultural concepts and artwork.

Could it be, I wondered, *that what I envisioned for the project was in fact a calling to go to Korea and actually implement the concept?* Was God saying to me that the promise of Acts 1:8 which had become quite literal with regard to Jerusalem, Judea, and Samaria was then literally going to be "the ends of the earth"? Korea? Yes, that to me was a calling and I determined to pursue it. Juanita was less convinced but willing to pray about it, and the children thought it might be a fun experience. The missionary was willing for us to come to Korea with a plan, provided I raised the $10,000.

In the summer of 1973, our family, which now included 18-month-old Danny, packed up and moved to Korea. My purpose for going to Korea for an extended period was to develop Sunday school material for the rapidly growing OMS-related denomination known as the Korean Evangelical Holiness Church (KEHC).

Our Korea experience was a tri-dimensional two-year adventure. There was the family experience, the mission or purpose experience, and my personal ministry experience – all against the backdrop of the Korean culture which, at that time, was still emerging from the devastation of the Korean War.

Having invested nearly three years on Okinawa in the Army, I had no problem dealing with the Korean culture. But in Korea I had my family with me and the added responsibility to sustain and protect each of them, while absorbing opportunities for experiences to broaden their worldview. Within two years I was able to design and produce the graded Sunday school materials, a Korean tract that was used to launch a nationwide "Great Day of Witness," and a series of ministry brochures for missionaries on furlough representing Korea.

With a temporary replacement in the OMS graphics department, I had planned a three-year short-term mission, and the possibility of a full four years in Korea. But medical issues with my replacement's wife cut our time to a little less than two years so we were called back to Greenwood. Fortunately, Jim Miles had continued to lead the Thursday Bible study group which served as our prayer team. I picked up where we had left off in the study and continued an additional 13 years.

Back at OMS

Our family returned to the OMS campus in the summer of 1975. I began interacting directly with the 12 fields of OMS, surveying their needs and suggesting literature to meet those needs, especially brochures for furlough and fundraising. Juanita began working in the student scholarship department at OMS. As with many homeland-based missionaries, our support account balance at OMS began to slip into the red, so I requested we take a 30 percent cut in allowance, and I would take on some graphic design projects for local clients.

From the late 1970s through the mid-1980s, I occupied a loaned space from a local architect in exchange for managing the office of Overseas Council for Seoul Theological Seminary. Overseas Council was raising scholarship and capital investment funds for the seminary. Juanita managed the scholarship funds as an extension of the OMS scholarship program. In that loaned space I was free to do graphic design and magazine layout work for OMS, while maintaining some select business accounts.

Relating to the Greenwood community as a graphic designer/businessman rather than as a missionary generated incredible opportunities for personal ministry. Within a few years I developed relationships that resulted in many coming to Christ – a real estate executive, the owner of a cabinet company, the owner of a printing company, a land developer, the owner of a hair salon and his wife, and others. There were many others who received a clear presentation of the Gospel but declined Christ's generous offer of salvation.

Praying for the World

In January 1985, I remember being at my drawing board and desk in the office, having a time of personal devotions. By then, I'd been consistently reading through the Bible for 13 years, so my faith in the Word and the Author of the Word had greatly increased. I was meditating on Mark 16:15: "Go into all the world and preach the Gospel to every creature." A familiar feeling swept over me that something profound was in the making as I wondered how anyone could fulfill the profound requirements of that simple command. How could I, or any one person for that matter, go everywhere and preach to every person on this planet – at that time, about 6.5 billion souls?

As I pondered the possibilities, I noticed a *Hammond Atlas* among the reference books on my desk. That particular version had not only all the maps of the world as well as the states of the U.S. and provinces of Canada, but also a listing of cities and the population of each.

An extraordinary prayer strategy began to take shape in my mind and heart. What if I committed to pray for every city in every country of the world then pray for the population of each country and city? It would obviously be a monumental investment of time and spiritual resolve to complete the task.

The prayer was simple, "Lord, bind every force in every country and city that opposes Your will and Word. Free every voice and force in every country and city that proclaims Your will and Word." I could reasonably assume that everywhere in the world where there were forces for good, there would likewise be forces for evil determined to oppose and destroy the good. So, in my overarching plan, the prayers were nothing less than warfare prayer.

Prayer through the *Hammond Atlas* took just shy of nine years, from January 1985 through November 1993. I couldn't escape the urge to pray around the world a second time, so I purchased a second atlas, a *Rand McNally*, which had similar features. Being more disciplined, I prayed through it from January 1994 through December 1998. A third time around the world with the same strategy took from January 2000 through December 2003. The fourth and final time was from April 2008 through December 2013.

Has that warfare prayer made a difference in the world? Who can say? When I began praying in 1985, the Berlin Wall was standing and the evil empire of the godless Soviet Union controlled much of Europe. When I finished the first circuit of prayer, all that had changed.

Ironically, the Berlin wall fell as I was praying through that part of the world. During my four virtual treks around the world, I would often take a cue from the news of the day and pray for the issues in that part of the world. I viewed conflicts in the news as mere symptoms and evidence of the devil and his minions at work. Those were battles I could suit up for and, in the full armor of God, enter into with faith. Warfare prayer has been an integral part of my ministry from the early days of 1985 to the present.

It should be noted that in spiritual warfare, there were battles with injuries and scars that often went unnoticed by the casual observer, wounds too deep to share. In those times, only the Word of God and His presence were sufficient to sustain and comfort. "He is my rock, and there is no unrighteousness in Him" (Psalm 92:15b).

Back to Full Time at OMS

In 1986 the contract that had reduced my OMS pay by 30 percent was canceled, and I returned to work full time in the OMS graphics department. The change of status at OMS meant I could no longer work out of the architect's office space. But I still had local clients I could service on evenings and weekends, so I moved my personal equipment into our home. For the next several years, things returned to normal. Eleanor Burr and I were once again producing the *Outreach* and *ACTION* magazines as well as brochures for both the homeland and the fields. I rebranded OMS with a new logo and updated the layout style of the magazines, incorporating the use of color throughout. It was not uncommon for OMS to win awards at annual Evangelical Press Association conferences.

To Russia with Love

In the early days of J.B. Crouse's stint as president, OMS partnered with other missionary organizations in CoMission*, a coalition to establish ministries in Russia. The old Soviet Union seemed to be collapsing, along with the Berlin wall, in 1991. The political barriers were temporarily down and the government seemed open to several types of educational programs, including a Christian seminary and teaching on business ethics from a Christian perspective. Also, teams of tourists were streaming into the country, many sponsored by the organizations of the coalition.

Juanita and I went with one of the teams in March and April of 1993, touring both Russia and Hungary. For me the experience was somewhat surreal. I was just finishing my first trek through the atlas and had recently prayed through those two countries. On a bus trip from Moscow to Vladimir, I was looking into the blank, expressionless faces of people along the road, and it struck me, "I have been here! I have prayed for you!"

I can't put into words the personal joy of walking among an entire nation of people with whom I shared a spiritual connection. Hungary was even more spiritually dark than Russia. Russia was godless after years of atheistic influence but Hungary, though seemingly more prosperous, was rife with spiritism and occult worship.

In 1999, as I was finishing my second trek through the world atlas, my prayers took on a warlike militancy against the evil that was driving the chaos in the world. The mantra was simple, "God is sovereign, the devil is not, and God answers prayer."

It seemed clear to me that intercessors could go on the offensive against the "spiritual wickedness in heavenly places" (Ephesians 6:12), so I began to prayerfully strategize against the source of evil rather than the symptoms and consequences of activity reflected in news reports and prayer letters. In simple terms, it was a ministry of warfare prayer. When I was in the presence of evil activity, that is, on the same battlefield with the enemy, it was tactical warfare prayer. If I was praying for situations influenced by evil forces from a distance, it was strategic warfare prayer.

Warfare Prayer

In July 1999, the MFM Cabinet was conducting its summer meeting in the MFM conference room. On the agenda was a project to build a new state-of-the-art facility for Radio 4VEH near Cap-Haitien, Haiti. With a stronger and wider radio signal, part of the plan called for the distribution of thousands of small solar-powered radios with a frequency fix-tuned to Radio 4VEH. It was indeed an ambitious and expensive plan.

It was determined that, along with an architectural, engineering, and funding endeavor, there should also be a serious prayer initiative to support the effort. I suppose because of my focused prayer for countries using an atlas, I was asked to consider serving as the Prayer Champion of the project. I promised to give the offer serious thought and prayer.

I left the meeting a bit uneasy because I knew something of the slave history and voodoo culture of the country, and prayer for Haiti would be well beyond typical reporting of prayer and praise notes. To accomplish anything of spiritual substance in a land perceived by many Haitian Christians to be formally dedicated to Satan in exchange for victory over the French in 1791 was going to require serious warfare prayer.

Was MFM ready for that?

Was I?

I went next door to the OMS World Intercessors office, the department that facilitates various OMS prayer programs. Lorna Chandler, the department's co-director, was there with Millie Janes, wife of an MFM Cabinet member. I laid out the offer and challenge I was facing. We prayed together for God's clear guidance in the matter, then I went home to check on a building project. We were adding a sunroom and an extension to the kitchen. The roof area had some temporary supports and was covered by a plastic tarp held down by a dozen or so long 2x4s.

It was a clear, sunny July day. Suddenly, without warning, the sky got black, a strong wind came up, lightning flashed, and a torrent of rain descended on our house. The 2x4s and the tarp went scattering into the neighbor's yard. I climbed a ladder to salvage something, anything, from the roof area and was suddenly knocked off the ladder.

I found myself flat on my back, covered with mud. As quickly as it had begun, the storm was over and the sun was again shining in a clear blue sky. I limped into the house and looked in the bathroom mirror. My 64-year-old face was muddy and my nose was bloody. My right arm and side were nearly immobile; they were severely bruised and remained purple and green for days.

As I stared stunned at the pathetic creature in the mirror, I could almost hear a taunting voice, "Do you really want to take me on in Haiti?"

Had more than 30 years in the Word and more than 10 years of warfare prayer experience led to this moment?

Had I just experienced what others referred to as a "power encounter?" I believe that is precisely what it was.

It occurred within the immediate vicinity of our home. No one even in the next block was apparently aware of the event. Yes, it was indeed spiritual warfare, up close and personal.

Plans for the new 4VEH facility, as well as the funding and prayer strategy, would be formalized at the winter MFM Cabinet meeting in Waco, Texas. I had a few months to pray, decide, and develop a plan. However, I was convinced that a prayer plan for Haiti would need to be offensive warfare prayer – that is, going on the attack against evil spiritual strongholds.

Cabinet Conference

In late 1999, Warren asked me to lead the morning devotions at the three days of the winter MFM Cabinet meetings, January 6-8, 2000, in Waco, Texas. I have never been comfortable with public speaking, and this assignment felt ill-timed. It meant I would be finishing the graphic design work on the next issue of *ACTION* magazine while working on a Haiti prayer plan, and now preparing three devotionals over the Christmas holidays.

I remember going into Velma Hardig's office, plopping into a seat, and lamenting, "Warren has just ruined my Christmas vacation." Velma, the consummate encourager, assured me that Warren had prayerfully considered other speakers and had not made the assignment lightly. Apparently, there were three messages to be voiced that only I could deliver. But what were they? From my growing reservoir of biblical understanding and maturing experience with true faith, what would God distill into three nuggets of devotional thought appropriate for the Cabinet agenda?

It is difficult for me to articulate what transpired in Waco during those three days. I had notes for three devotionals but after opening remarks, the sessions seemed to flow far beyond my preparation and abilities. It was like I, too, was a spectator to the events.

On Thursday, January 6, I spoke of places of remembrance. The landscape of the Old Testament was marked with altars, places where God had met His people in special ways. Likewise, the landscape of each of our lives is marked with events and places where God has met us in special ways, and our faith and confidence to face daunting challenges before us is perhaps best found in revisiting those places.

On Friday, January 7, I spoke of God's remarkable method of provision, and His seeming disregard for logic and basic math: five loaves and two fish fed more than 5,000 people. I quoted the incredible statistics from the U.S. Army Quartermaster concerning what was needed to sustain more than 2 million people for 40 years in the most hostile environment on the planet. When we surrender to God, what we have is *everything* we need to accomplish God's mission before us.

I still can't articulate what happened the morning of Saturday, January 8, 2000. I was concerned that my notes for the devotional were disorganized and incomplete. I wanted to say something about a prayer initiative in Haiti in support of the Radio 4VEH building project, which was featured on the agenda for the day. I wanted to speak about spiritual opposition the projected new voice of 4VEH would encounter. I wanted to emphasize that the true challenge in Haiti was not the voice of radio going forth, but the spiritual deafness of the masses; unstopping the ears of Haitians would require binding the work of the devil in Haiti. It would mean serious spiritual combat.

From the old maps and atlases I had prayed through, I believed there were six provinces in Haiti, and the population was about six million people. I wanted to confirm that, so at breakfast I asked OMS executive Dr. David Dick to check it out on his laptop computer.

Although the hotel's Wi-Fi was not responding at that moment, he promised to keep trying.

Later, as I walked forward to speak, David handed me the torn corner from an envelope. On it were scribbled the words, "There are nine administrative districts in Haiti."

I told the Cabinet group, consisting of about 33 men, most of whom had also been at the previous summer meeting in Greenwood, that I had been asked to consider being the prayer champion for the Radio 4VEH project in Haiti. Then I related a bit of Haiti's slave history and how they obtained independence over the French.

In 1791, voodoo witch doctors in a sacred ceremony killed a pig, drank its blood and purportedly promised Satan that if he would deliver them from French domination, they would dedicate Haiti to him for 200 years. There was a revolution, victory, and ultimately independence in 1804. The clock was ticking toward a 200th anniversary in 2004 and the declaration of Haiti's president to rededicate the country to another 200 years of allegiance to Satan.

My appeal was simple. The scope of a prayer initiative in Haiti would need to go far beyond the Radio 4VEH project. It would need to challenge demonic forces and strongholds that bound Haitian hearts and minds in every province of the country.

Then I drew an outline of Haiti on a white board and roughly sketched in the nine administrative districts, which I referred to as "sectors," a military designation. The evil strongholds in each sector needed to be identified and challenged with offensive warfare prayer. I felt each sector needed to be literally stepped on and claimed, and that prayer warriors involved in the battle needed to be surrounded by support intercessors. It was going to be a spiritual battle fought independently of the radio project but ultimately in support of it, as evil forces would be bound and people were enabled to hear and respond to the radio voice.

My closing was short and blunt. I can't recall the exact wording, but I told how I had been asked at the last Cabinet meeting to head up the prayer initiative in Haiti.

"Gentlemen," I said, "I am willing to lead the charge if there are nine men willing to take responsibility for each of the nine sectors. With heads up and eyes wide open, are there nine men who will stand with me?"

Instantly, nine men were on their feet – not eight, not ten, but nine!

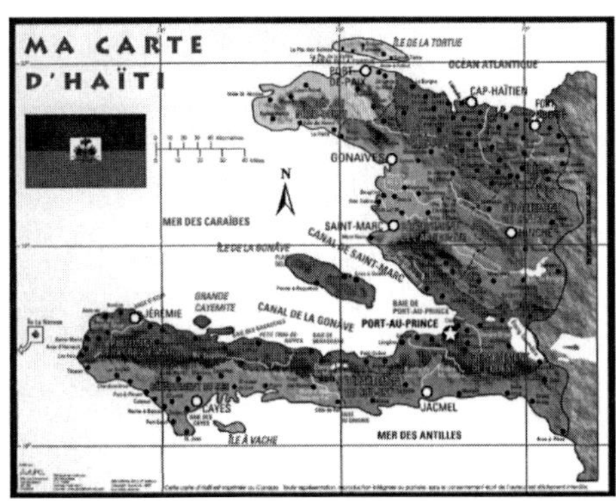

Map as outlined by Gene Bertolet to capture the 9 individual sectors which the Holy Spirit led through 9 men.

I was visibly stunned, and so was everyone in the room. We silently surrounded the nine men who had been prompted by the Holy Spirit and prayerfully commissioned them to the spiritual battle that lay ahead. Then, we spontaneously broke into song, *I have decided to follow Jesus ... no turning back ... no turning back.* It was indeed a holy moment!

I left Waco with nine names and corresponding e-mail addresses. I looked at them on the plane trip back to Indianapolis and wondered, *What next?* I really didn't have a follow-up plan because I hadn't developed a strategy to go to war in Haiti, nor had I planned to appeal for volunteers to join me in the battle. I recalled the muddy, bloody reflection in the mirror the previous July and the haunting question, "Do you really want to take me on in Haiti?" This was the moment of truth. Was I willing to lead these nine men into spiritual warfare against an entrenched enemy in Haiti, knowing they, too, would face the enemy's wrath? Suddenly I had a nine-man team awaiting orders for deployment: surely the God of Saturday's devotional had a plan for our next steps in Haiti.

A promise God made to Moses and Joshua concerning the conquest of Canaan resonated with my spirit concerning the challenge before us in Haiti: "Every place on which the sole of your foot treads, shall be yours; I have given it to you, just as I spoke to Moses" (Deuteronomy 11:24; Joshua 1:3).

Wayne King was one of the nine men who stood when I appealed for volunteers in Waco. I told him I felt strongly that I should go to Haiti and personally place the sole of my foot on each of the nine sectors before I sent each of the sector leaders to do likewise. He agreed. So the following month, February 2000, Wayne and I flew to Haiti and teamed with Emmanuel Felix, a devout Haitian brother who is well versed in voodoo and spiritual warfare. Together, we visited the most notorious voodoo sites in northern Haiti – the tree under which Haiti was dedicated to Satan in 1791, which was still lush and green; and the polluted Pool of St. Jacques, where voodoo worshipers come from all over Haiti to bathe, drink, and participate in voodoo rituals.

On the narrow gravel road to the tree, we passed under a banner. Emmanuel translated where it advertised the coming rededication of Haiti to Satan for another 200 years.

We surrounded the tree, placed our hands on its thorny bark and prayed against the evil influence it represented and against the Haiti president's plan to perpetuate Satan's "legal" right to Haiti. I must admit, at that very moment I felt we were picking a fight with overwhelming evil forces in Haiti, a fight we couldn't simply turn and walk away from. It would require sustained and fervent offensive warfare prayer coupled with divine guidance and protection. Everyone associated with the Haiti Prayer Initiative would need to be surrounded with a circle of supporting, serious, fervent intercessors.

Wayne contracted with Missionary Flights to charter a small plane for the day to fly us to an airstrip in each of the nine sectors. In the spirit of Joshua 1:3, I "set the sole of my foot" on every sector as I stepped off the plane, claimed each sector for Christ, and gathered two rocks: a small one for a master prayer map in Greenwood (the very map I held as we charted the path of the survey trip) and a larger rock to be retained in a memorial heap (see Joshua 4:3). Emmanuel was skeptical at first, but soon gathered prayer rocks for himself. The circuit of Haiti and the sectors took nearly all day. The sun was setting and the Cap-Haitien airport closed at dark, so for the last sector in northeast Haiti near the Dominican border, we had to settle for a close flyover.

However, in 2001, I returned to Haiti and made a trip with Emmanuel to that sector to officially step on it, claim it for Christ, and gather the rocks.

After the survey trip, I returned to Greenwood with a clear view of all of Haiti from the air (which looked exactly like the map I held on the flight). I had photos of each sector's main airstrip and nearby dwellings and people, the rocks, and an emerging warfare prayer strategy to attempt to wrestle Haiti from the enemy's grasp.

I had already determined that being the Prayer Champion for the Radio 4VEH project was far too limited. The battle in Haiti was not primarily building and maintaining the strong radio voice of 4VEH, it was binding evil forces that dulled the ears and hearts of millions of Haitians to spiritual truth. Thus, the Haiti Prayer Initiative was for all of Haiti, all nine sectors. And once started, the battle would need to be sustained apart from and well beyond the construction phase of the new 4VEH facility and radio distribution.

The inspiration for an offensive strategy against the entrenched evil strongholds in Haiti came from Mark 3:22-27. After Jesus cast out a demon, He was accused of being a minion of Satan.

His response is noteworthy: "How can Satan cast out Satan? If a kingdom is divided against itself, that kingdom cannot stand. If a house is divided against itself, that house will not be able to stand. If Satan has risen up against himself and is divided, he cannot stand, but he is finished! No one can enter the strong man's house and plunder his property unless he first binds the strong man, and then he will plunder his house."

In that brief passage, I discovered the strategy and battle cry for our looming offensive in Haiti: "Divide, Bind, and Plunder Satan's Strongholds." This would truly be a battle for the very soul of Haiti.

The spiritual demographic of Haiti placed most of the sacred voodoo sites in the northern part of the country. The central region was mountainous and less populated. The capital city of Port-au-Prince was the most populated and was also home of Haiti's president, who was determined to keep Haiti in Satan's grip. The southern tier of the sectors seemed to be less dominated by voodoo, though all of Haiti is permeated by the influence of the religion.

I realized that if we were able to impact Haiti's voodoo strongholds with offensive warfare prayer, there would doubtless be counterattacks from the enemy. With that in mind, I assigned the top five sectors to older men who demonstrated spiritual maturity and had grown children. I assigned the sector with the infamous tree and polluted pool – Ground Zero for the Prayer Initiative – to Wayne King. I assigned Harry Burr the capital city, because of his many trips to Haiti leading MFM teams and his knowledge of Haiti's history and culture. The bottom tier sectors seemed to be less corrupted with zealous voodoo worship and sacred sites, and I assigned them to younger men with small children, hoping to mitigate some of the enemy's possible counterattacks.

I e-mailed each of the sector leaders with instructions for claiming their respective sectors for Christ:

1. Surround themselves with a circle of serious, experienced intercessors.
2. Visit their assigned sector as soon as possible, step on it, claim it for Christ, and pick up a rock as a personal memorial.
3. Identify the major spiritual strongholds and centers of evil influence in their sector.
4. Daily pray over their map – for every city and village in their sector – that every evil influence be bound and every influence for righteousness be loosed and empowered.
5. As prayerful instruction for warfare prayer, read Wesley Duewel's book, *Mighty Prevailing Prayer*, which I enclosed for each of them.

At the Greenwood MFM office, I organized a Tuesday noon warfare prayer group to support the nine sector leaders and their penetration into Haiti, and to pray for the Radio 4VEH construction project. Another prayer priority at that time was funding for the acquisition of quality solar-powered radios, fix-tuned to 4VEH, for distribution in Haiti.

The Tuesday Haiti prayer group met until 2016. In the early days of the meetings, 20 to 30 intercessors, often on their knees, participated in fervent warfare prayer. There were reports of incredible changes in Haiti – the tree was dying, and witch doctors were coming to Christ. The best news was that, rather than rededicating Haiti to Satan, Haiti's president was deposed and found himself exiled in Africa, and the new president was open to Christianity and spiritual changes. It was an incredible time for MFM and for the many who accepted the challenge to exercise warfare prayer on behalf of Haiti.

After our survey trip to Haiti, Wayne King had an idea for raising funds for the solar-powered radios. We were eating lunch at a local Burger King in Greenwood when he floated the idea that perhaps a cartoonish character could appeal to kids and invite them to sponsor radios. I agreed the plan might have possibilities.

So, on the back of a Burger King placemat, I sketched a boxy character with a stylized solar panel, sunglasses, and a microphone. For a bit of personal flavor, I added a caricature of Wayne's face. He loved it!

We went to work designing an entire kid-friendly campaign around the new sun-powered missionary we named "Sonny Solar." Wayne suggested Sonny could be a spokesperson for radio sponsorships who could go to Sunday school classes, VBS, camps, etc. Actually, the proposed campaign suddenly grew to include churches, missionary conferences, and even community events. I created the design layouts for postcards, posters, buttons, balloons, monogramed sunglasses, and small radio-shaped boxes to collect cash to purchase the solar radios.

Wayne then asked me to design a Sonny mascot outfit that he could wear at special events. I fabricated it out of two-inch-thick foam rubber sheets and added huge sunglasses and, of course, a solar panel. Wayne and I worked on the math for the number of fix-tuned solar radios we hoped to fund for all of Haiti. Working with the demographics published in *Operation World*, we determined it would take 250,000 radios to saturate all nine sectors of Haiti. If the 250,000 radios were sponsored at $30 each, more than $7.5 million dollars would need to be raised – enough to fund the new 4VEH broadcast center, radios, marketing, and some future operating expenses. Wayne and I developed a funding plan for the Haiti Radio Project we hoped the Cabinet would find acceptable and approve at the next MFM Cabinet meeting.

When the MFM Cabinet met in July 2000, there was great excitement. The prayer initiative had taken on a life of its own. Things were happening in Haiti that could only be regarded as coincidence or the result of warfare prayer. Even veteran missionaries began to take notice. Wayne was ready with a well-devised plan to fund the new broadcast center and fix-tuned solar radios, as well as the marketing plan.

Several things happened at the Cabinet meeting that were unprecedented in OMS and MFM history. The MFM Cabinet and the OMS Board, which was also meeting elsewhere on campus, approved the plan and assigned it an official project number to receive donations. Also at the meeting, I presented a proposal that the project be named *Operation Saturation* (OpSat) because the goals were to saturate Haiti with the 4VEH radio frequency, saturate the radio waves with the Gospel, saturate Haiti with solar radios fix-tuned to the 4VEH frequency, and saturate Haiti with warfare prayer to hinder Satan's opposition to the plan. Wayne was appointed director of marketing for the project and given a percent of all raised funds for a marketing budget; he immediately began to produce the cardboard box banks, posters, postcards, Sonny Solar trinkets for kids, and the famous Sonny outfit.

Sonny Solar, the character which originated from Gene Bertolet's napkin drawing to raise funds for the solar-powered, fix-tuned station, Radio 4VEH.

MFM approved the plan as an official funding project. Normally, MFM projects were for one year, but *Operation Saturation* was given five years. That changed the way I handled the marketing and reported the project in *ACTION* magazine. Too much was happening in Haiti to report in the magazine, and other fields of OMS needed to be fairly represented. So I proposed a separate newsletter-style publication, devoted exclusively to the Haiti project, to be published in between the quarterly *ACTION* mailings. The newsletter, which I named *Inter-ACTION*, began publication in 2001 and ran for the duration of the project. As the project was promoted and reported in publications and marketing materials were mailed out, funds began to pour in to underwrite new construction, equipment, and fix-tuned radios.

I should probably share some deep concerns I had related to *Operation Saturation*. From that traumatic muddy, bloody day in July 1999, I focused on the seriousness of warfare prayer, and the potential high cost of a spiritual battle for the very soul of Haiti. Assuming the responsibility for the spiritual lives, and perhaps fortunes, of nine men added to the burden.

It was spiritually rewarding to witness dramatic changes in Haiti as the nine sector leaders, our Tuesday Haiti prayer meeting, and circles of intercessors across the country actually engaged the enemy in Haiti in spiritual combat. The battle was brutal at times. One sector leader's daughter, a missionary in Africa, was killed in a freak car accident. Another sector leader nearly lost his business livelihood, another went virtually blind, and still another developed cancer and died. Juanita developed a rash and itch in 1999 that has never yet been diagnosed or successfully treated.

In my view, all nine paid a price, though I'm aware that some issues may have been coincidental and had little or nothing to do with their involvement in the prayer initiative. I should also note that while warfare prayer intercessors were literally on their knees before God engaged in real spiritual combat against the real enemy, obvious and profound changes occurred in Haiti.

Years later, as prayers became typical and more focused on symptoms, the enemy continued to prevail and advance. It reminded me of the story in Exodus 17 as Joshua was battling the Amalekites while Moses was perched on a hill overlooking the battle. When Moses' hands were raised in intercession, Joshua prevailed. When Moses' hands grew weary and went limp, the enemy prevailed. Fortunately for all, Aaron and Hur came alongside Moses and held up his hands until victory was achieved. We brothers held each other up, as did our intercessors.

In keeping with the MFM Cabinet's mandated five-year limit for the 4VEH Radio Project and likewise a supposed limit on the prayer initiative, I officially wrapped it up, five years to the hour. It officially began Saturday, January 8, 2000, in Waco, Texas, at the MFM Cabinet meeting; five years later, again in Waco, on Saturday, January 8, 2005, I was again leading morning devotions. Five years earlier the messages were looking with faith into an uncertain future. In 2005,

I delivered the same devotions looking back with praise to God for what He had done through the nine sector leaders and the many who had fervently interceded. Each of the nine had gathered a stone from Haiti on their initial visit to claim their sector, and we piled them in the center of the table as a memorial, inspired by Levites gathering memorial stones from the Jordan River as they stepped into the Promised Land (Joshua 4:3).

During the days of *Operation Saturation*, I developed and produced a Level-1 Warfare Prayer Manual intended as basic training for those desiring to be part of the MFM Warfare Prayer Initiative. It outlined in military terms the basics of the Christian faith and focused on tactical and strategic prayer for challenging and neutralizing an enemy stronghold. The overarching theme was that every true believer is in a real war with a real enemy determined to destroy his or her faith.

One of the opening statements read, "Spiritual warfare is usually thought of in terms of defense and protecting oneself, loved ones, and possessions from the devil's attacks. Rarely these days is it considered in terms of offensive, preemptive, and sustained actions against the devil's strongholds. The ultimate weapon in such strikes is warfare prayer!"

The summary concluding statement read, "Those wandering around the battlefield as unprotected, unprepared soldiers, or curious spectators, believing it's someone else's war, will likely become casualties or prisoners of the enemy. Now is the time to step up and side with the One who broke Satan's power at Calvary, sealed his doom, and predetermined the outcome of this battle. 'We fight not for victory but from the position of victory' –Wesley Duewel." This Level-1 manual is available from MFM.

Later, I produced a Level-4 Warfare Prayer Manual intended only for those who fully embraced the basics of Level-1 and were prepared to fully engage the enemy in warfare prayer. That proved to be a relatively small but tough band of seasoned prayer warriors. For those, the Level-4 Manual included Level-1 and added Level-2, which involved preparation and strategies for taking on multiple strongholds on a given battlefield. Haiti, with its nine sectors, was a prime example. Level-3 dealt with strategies for challenging the demonic forces that directly influenced or controlled strongholds. Level-4 explored the opportunities and potential for praying without ceasing and experiencing lifestyle intercession. The first printing of the Level-4 Manual was dedicated to the memory of my dad, who was affectionately known as "Pastor Earl" among MFMers who knew him well. He and Mom were especially known in Haiti where they had spent months – Dad training Haitians to use broom-making equipment he had shipped in, and Mom making outfits for children. The first edition of warfare prayer, covering Levels 1-4, is available by contacting Men for Missions.

Today, thanks to MFM's continued involvement, over a hundred homes were built for 2010 earthquake victims. Radio 4VEH is not only broadcasting on the radio, but is on television as well.

All praise to the Lord!

**See the Glossary for a description of flannel-graphs, Nav's Topical Memory System and CoMission.*

Indonesia and Nancy Gill

Warren Hardig

"How blessed is the man who finds wisdom and the man who gains understanding" (Proverbs 3:13).

On my first trip to Haiti, I experienced firsthand the power of a layman giving a witness of how Jesus can come into the life of an individual and change that life. The same Holy Spirit who raised Jesus from the dead can change the life of a common man anywhere – in an office, a garage, or a farm chemical business.

Even if the witness is given through an interpreter, the Holy Spirit can communicate the message of salvation with convicting power. He is not hindered by any cultural, racial, or linguistic barrier. "And God, who knows the heart, bore witness to them, giving them the Holy Spirit, just as He also did to us and He made no distinction between us and them, cleansing their hearts by faith" (Acts 15:8-9).

Participants on Men for Missions ministry teams have been privileged to meet many great men and women who have dedicated all they have to Jesus. One of those missionaries was Nancy Gill, a lady from Northern Ireland serving in Indonesia.

The team I led to the South Pacific split up on Sunday morning in order to observe and participate in different worship services. Nancy had hired a vehicle to transport us to the congregation where I would tell how Jesus had changed my life.

Our transportation was a motorized tricycle belching out fumes from a motor fueled by gasoline and oil. We joined a multitude of similar vehicles, all of them leaving great clouds of blue smoke, which made it difficult to breathe and quite challenging to arrive at the church clean. Our lungs managed to give us just enough oxygen to survive the ride to a home where a young pastor and his wife greeted us with great enthusiasm.

People began to gather around us. We sang hymns, listened to a Scripture reading and some general announcements, then I was introduced. Nancy translated my testimony as I explained how I, a simple man in the farm chemical business, had been afraid to grow old and die, and I didn't know what to do in church. However, when I knelt to pray at a fertilizer business, I found peace, deliverance, and new life in Christ.

Through Nancy's translation and with music playing, I invited the congregation to come forward if they would like to experience forgiveness of their sins. The singing of the hymn was beautiful, but we heard the sound of weeping even over the music. Three ladies were sitting together and crying uncontrollably, which immediately caught our attention.

The crowd left except for the three ladies, who told us they had had an encounter with a witch doctor who cast a spell on them, causing each of them to be more desirous of him rather than to their husbands. As they came forward, Nancy began to talk with them. The pastor and his wife were included and, over the next two or three hours, Nancy, who was single, with the Lord's guidance, plunged into intense spiritual warfare, leading the three ladies to salvation and deliverance.

It was midafternoon before we left for home in our smoke-belching vehicle and, as I thought about the events that morning, I thanked

God for His provision in bringing someone like Nancy to this country. I am still moved by the events that morning, and remember how faithfully Nancy served, loved the people of Indonesia, and is now buried there.

"Come and hear, all who fear God, and I will tell of what He has done for my soul" (Psalm 66:16).

Experiences in Colombia

Warren Hardig

The most fulfilling days for Men for Missions are when we are directly involved with men and women, especially those of another culture, telling them about Christ's goodness.

In July 2012, MFM officially began supporting the Every Community for Christ (ECC) evangelistic and church planting movement initiated in Bogota, Colombia, called *Satura Colombia* in connection with Doug and Cindy Tankersley. We began by sending evangelism teams who would help train the church locals while providing them a boost of encouragement to evangelize among their own people.

MFM first began sending two or three teams a year in 2012. Beginning in 2015, the numbers of teams began to increase. This was largely due to prayer by the Colombians based on Luke 10:2 and Mathew 9:37-38, as well as MFM now having their own full-time missionaries on the field. In addition, MFM short-term members were returning home and sharing an awareness of how ripe the fields were for harvest, including the need to send additional laborers. The number of teams quickly increased to about 10 per year.

In March 2017, the MFM team had the opportunity to participate in Sunday morning worship and four days of door-to-door evangelism, giving testimony of Christ's love, goodness, and salvation. It was my privilege to be on this trip. My interpreter and I walked together, watching for people we could approach.

I prayed with an expectant mother who had her young daughter by her side while people passed by. I told a young man how Jesus had given me salvation, deliverance, and taken away the fear of dying. I asked if he would pray and ask Jesus into his life, and he prayed while two of his friends watched from a short distance on their motorcycles. My interpreter told me they were drug dealers.

A knock on one door was answered by someone who did not step out to be clearly seen. She was willing to hear my story, and I told her about being a shy country boy who grew up afraid to get old and die. I told her about how I began to attend church. I told her of my addiction to tobacco and how one morning I prayed and asked God to forgive my sins and to take tobacco away from me.

Her response was, "I have cancer in my throat because I smoke."

My heart grieved for her. I told her how clean I felt after my prayer and how God delivered me from my addiction.

The lady responded, "I have breast cancer, also."

My response was, "Ma'am, I would never do anything that would hurt you. Yet I must ask whether you are ready for wherever this cancer is going to take you?"

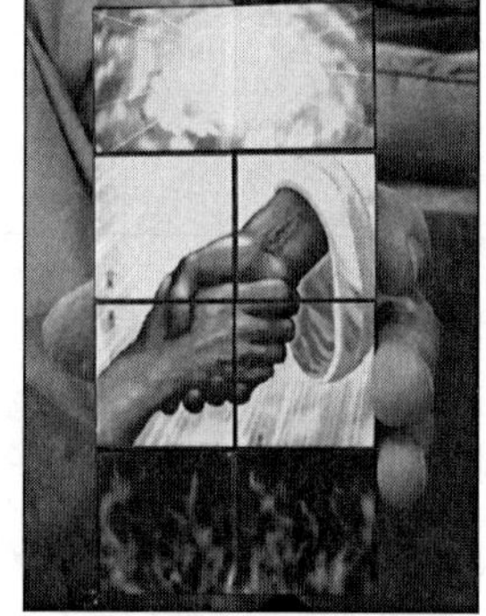

She shook her head "No."

I asked my Colombian brother to share the plan of salvation using the EvangeCube™* *(as shown)*. After she prayed to receive Christ, I asked if she had a Bible. Again, she shook her head "No."

I told her, "Men for Missions in Canada would like to give you one in your own language," and she received the Word of God. My interpreter and I both wiped away tears as we said our goodbyes.

After leaving her house, we ran into two teenage girls who were on the way home from school. When I finished giving my testimony, which always included my admission that I had been afraid to get old and die, one of the young ladies said, "I am afraid to get old, and I am afraid to die."

I responded, "You stick with me and we're going to take care of that."

They eagerly prayed and asked Jesus to forgive them and take away their fears. I will never forget the way the girls skipped joyfully away after giving their hearts to Jesus!

When I came back to my home church the first Sunday morning, I found it tough because I kept seeing the faces of all the people we had talked to on our trip. Particularly I kept seeing the face of the lady with cancer from smoking.

What if we had not gone? What about those we did not have time to see?

I am now like other MFMers who have a favorite city: I want to go back to Medellín to see people we met – Carlos, Francis, Camila, and the pastors – and meet some we didn't have time to see.

The wonderful news is that by March 1, 2020, MFM had sent 40 short-term evangelism teams to Colombia with 322 short-term team members and had seen more than 15,333 people make personal decisions to accept Jesus as their Lord and Savior. It is unknown how many more have heard the Gospel from these new believers because they have excitedly continued to share the Gospel with their friends, family, and neighbors. This number of decisions does not even factor in the roughly 160 churches MFM helped to train during this time and are now out today continuing to share the Gospel and train others to do the same.

Being a pioneer for God means your heart will frequently break and the message must be shared because you can see people who need Jesus. He walks with us every step of the way, puts hope in our hearts and His own tender love in our words. Trusting Him is the only way to live this life.

**See the Glossary for more information on the EvangeCube.*

Following God's Leading

Warren Hardig

John Schultz was serious about his prayer life. He always prayed for the Lord's guidance wherever he was. Once, while waiting in the terminal before his flight, he knew the Lord was leading him to sit next to a particular man.

"I've just been asking the Lord where to sit and he directed me to you," John said to him. "Do you have any idea why?"

The man was quick to respond. "My son is on trial for murder and I'm flying to be by his side. I was just praying, asking the Lord, 'Isn't there someone you can send to pray with me?'"

See, that's how the Lord works …

"Many plans are in a man's heart, but the counsel of the Lord will stand. What is desirable in a man is his kindness; it is better to be a poor man than a liar" (Proverbs 19:21-22).

God's Healing to Warren

Velma Hardig

In 1986, Warren was working alongside Jack Goodbrand with Men for Missions Councils in Ontario, Canada, when he became very ill with stomach pain. After arriving home in Greenwood, Indiana, a few days later, Warren visited several specialists and underwent many examinations to determine the cause of the worsening illness – but they found nothing.

Approximately 10 to 14 days later, I took Warren to the emergency room. Something was dreadfully wrong. He was examined again, and this time was diagnosed with a severe case of diverticulitis. They admitted him to the hospital, where his condition continued to worsen.

That Tuesday, OMS International had its regularly scheduled half-day of prayer, which I had planned to attend before going to the hospital to be with Warren. However, while I was getting ready that morning, the Lord impressed me to go to the hospital early. Just before I left, Warren called for me to come be with him because he felt so bad.

When I arrived at his room, he was pale and perspiration was running off him as though someone had turned on a faucet. Immediately I asked a nurse to take his temperature. She told me that one-half hour earlier his temperature was 103 degrees and had been that way all night. However, as a way to comfort us, she took his temperature again and it had dropped to 101 degrees. She was amazed. Warren's temperature continued to fall.

I can tell you why it fell so radically: during the prayer time at OMS, the missionaries that morning prayed for Warren very specifically. Dr. Wesley Duewel asked everyone to open their Bibles and put their hands on James 5:14-15 as he prayed for Warren's healing: "Is anyone among you sick? Then he must call for the elders of the church and they are to pray over him, anointing him with oil in the name of the Lord; and the prayer offered in faith will restore the one who is sick, and the Lord will raise him up, and if he has committed sins, they will be forgiven him."

For some reason, missionary Bob Wood noted the time Dr. Duewel did this; so did I, and later he and I compared times of the temperature drop with the prayer for healing. They coincided exactly. Warren's condition was so severe, he remained in the hospital two weeks for further treatment and rest. And his recovery was incredibly good!

I discussed this situation several years later with the Christian doctor who had cared for Warren through this difficult time. I told him the above account. He asked me why I had not told him before, because the blood counts taken that very day showed Warren's white blood count had fallen 20,000 points. For years the doctor thought the hospital had made a mistake with that blood test, because radical white blood counts just don't fall that drastically. The physician realized a miracle had taken place in the middle of medical treatment. So, there is documented evidence of God's miracle in Warren's medical records.

We praise the Lord for His goodness and will always give Him praise for His protection and healing in Warren's life.

HERE AM I, SEND ME

Carl Poynter

Introduction by Warren Hardig

"One who is gracious to a poor man lends to the Lord, and He will repay him for his good deed" (Proverb 19:17).

Carl Poynter has helped more than 100 Haitian families who lost their homes in a devastating earthquake. Standing with him were his precious wife, Teresa, and their two sons. Carl and Teresa are Christians with a global ministry who have served the Lord faithfully in Japan and Haiti, and continue to do so wherever the Lord leads them.

Carl's drive and motivation are fueled by his devotional life. He hides God's word in his heart, enabling him to give an account of his faith, whether privately or in a crowd. Carl's work ethic and winsome personality draw men from all walks of life to be part of Men for Missions, and his compassionate heart fuels his message about the needs of those who cannot represent themselves. As an ambassador of Jesus Christ, he communicates a compelling challenge for everyone who knows Christ to get involved. For those who don't know Him, Carl lays it on the line: *Christ died for your sins. Accept Him today.* Hear his story, in his own words …

I grew up in a wonderful family in Vandalia, Ohio – Mom, Dad, and my younger brother, Clay. We had a great family life and were taught high moral standards, hard work, and strong life values. Although we believed in God and Jesus, we were not a family who went to church. One day when I was about 13, Brother John Vader from the local Baptist church showed up on our doorstep to invite our family to come to church. My parents rejected going at that time, but asked us boys if we wanted to go. I said "Yes" … and early seeds began being planted in my life.

I soon dedicated my life to Jesus through repentance and joined the AWANA* Club for boys. It was the church's version of the Boy Scouts, where we earned rewards and arrowhead pins for memorizing and reciting Bible verses. That came very easy for me, because God had already equipped me with gifts for future endeavors I did not yet know about.

When I was 16 or 17, I no longer had an interest in church; my attention turned to sports, girls, fast cars, and hanging out with friends … which led me down a long, dark road of partying, drinking, and doing drugs.

My wife Teresa was my high school sweetheart. My life was so out of control, I am still not sure why she put up with me and all my shenanigans – but I'm thankful she did. After our first child, Curtis, was born in 1989, I began turning back around. I had a great job where I made tons of money, but more importantly, our family started attending church together in 2001. We were blessed with another son, Justin, in 2002. Both boys are now grown.

Soon after I returned to church, God spoke to me on Easter morning 2001. I ran to the altar, repented of all my sins, and had a real born-again experience, then I was baptized.

We still attend the same church today, Northridge Freewill Baptist in Dayton, Ohio. My relationship with the Lord really became serious in 2009 when I said to God: "I have failed you so many times, but I am ready to surrender all to serve you, Lord. Here am I, send me."

To my utter surprise, He was not only listening, but He had much, much more waiting for me.

My life-changing journey actually began on a mission trip with Men for Missions the day after Thanksgiving, 2009. I had committed to a two-week trip to an orphanage in Jeremie, Haiti, for what would be my first international missions trip.

I went with fellow church member John Barber, who was an associate staff member of MFM, and Gene Pollic, an MFM regional director. Little did I realize how this trip would completely transform my future plans.

Although I considered myself a solid Christian, I was also a successful businessman earning a large salary, driving a company vehicle, dining at the finest restaurants, playing golf with clients, and vacationing well with my family. I had new cars in the garage and was chasing money and the American dream. I returned from Haiti a totally different person, a changed man who lost all desire for worldly riches. While I was in Haiti, God put a calling on my life to forsake all and follow Him, just as He invites us all in Matthew 4:19, "'Come, follow me,' Jesus said." In doing so, He broke my heart for Haiti.

On January 12, 2010, a month after I returned home, a great earthquake struck Haiti. I took several trips to Haiti that year, and even led a couple of teams focused on building an orphanage, installing water filtration units, and helping with the 7.0 earthquake's aftermath. In early 2010, Teresa and I applied to be full-time missionaries with OMS. To our surprise, in a short couple of months, we were accepted as career missionaries and invited to move our family, including our two young boys, to Spain.

As I reflect on this, I can say our life was thrown directly into a whirlwind, something much bigger than us and something only God could do. We began traveling the U.S., raising funds for our ministry and seeking prayer partners. To keep costs down, our family lived out of a van, staying in our tent at campgrounds, and being guests in many people's homes, allowing us to live a life of faith as an example to our boys. We took several trips to Spain, only to have God change our course mid-stream. During our two years of funding and traveling the states, I found myself back in Haiti every couple of months.

In November 2012, I was approached by Kent Eller, MFM National Director, who asked me to consider becoming a regional director for the U.S. Northeast. What got my attention most was when Kent said, "You do realize the world is much larger than just Haiti, don't you?"

Kent wasn't telling us not to go to Haiti. Instead, he was saying, "If you are willing to *Do, Go, and Give* yourself, God can and will use you in many other places along with Haiti."

I accepted that role with Men for Missions and am now going into my ninth year as a regional director, which has been such a blessing. I have had the privilege not only to travel the U.S. and go to Spain a couple of times, but I have also taken multiple teams to Haiti, Colombia, Japan, and the Dominican Republic.

One of the greatest blessings for our family was when we lived in Haiti in 2015-2016, where we hosted teams and were trusted with leading the construction of the Bon Repos church project, along with being one of the construction team leaders for Homes for Haiti. In 2018 we had the opportunity to move to northern Haiti to help with the Cowman School project, named after Charles Cowman, who originated OMS. What an honor!

A dear Men for Missions brother, Tex Clark, said to me, "God doesn't care about your abilities, He cares about your availability."

Is God calling you? Will you be available?

I encourage you to say to Him what I said years ago, "Here am I, Lord, send me!"

You may not know what He has in store for you, but He will be with you every step of your incredible life-changing journey.

**See the Glossary for a description of AWANA Club.*

School #35 Will Never be the Same

Warren Hardig

"He who gives to the poor will never want, but he who shuts his eyes will have many curses" (Proverbs 28:27).

As I read Proverbs 28:27, I began to pray for the Moscow Evangelical Christian Seminary, and all the students and faculty, like Sasha, Natasha, Julia, Sergey, and Nina.

In my mind, I am walking across Red Square watching the folks pouring into Lenin's tomb and the elderly ladies sitting on small stools begging for help. I am then riding down the longest and fastest escalator I have ever been on, looking at a myriad of people, including *babushkas* (older ladies) bundled up in dark, heavy clothes, pushing their few meager belongings in a small cart. The basket of one cart contains barley that has somehow managed to survive the ride. They struggle to get their belongings on and off the escalator.

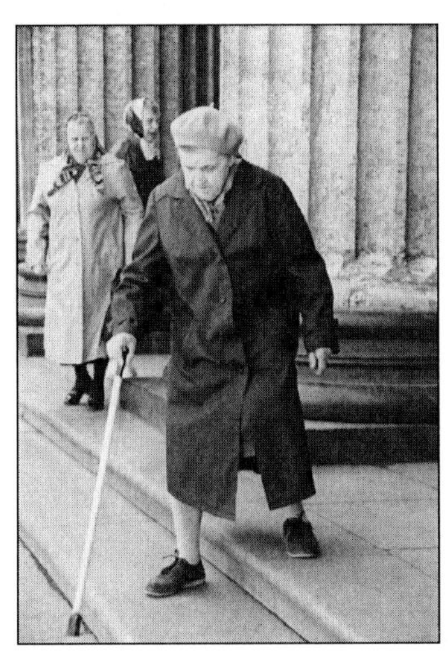

More than once, I take hold of their precious belongings in an act of help, ignoring their protests as they were too small and too weak to stop me. When we stop at the exit, I give them back their carts. The language barrier persists, but the language from their hearts I see through their eyes is a reward far greater than my small effort.

Giving to the poor can happen in many ways, and the reward is priceless. One little boy gifted me with a broken syringe as a small act of kindness. Going into schools, having children give us handmade gifts, and making the friends we did in Russia can't be described with pen and paper.

In the years of the CoMission*, I was able to lead 12 teams to Russia and other countries of the former Soviet Union. Though I was never deployed into fighting in the U.S. Army during the Cold War, Vietnam War, Berlin Wall crisis, or the Cuban Missile Crisis, I entered Russia with a cynical attitude. The barbed wire I saw the first time we deboarded the plane confirmed the stories I had been told years before of what Russia was like.

I would look around and see ladies sweeping snow with crude stick brooms on Red Square. I found out that the average woman in Russia underwent 10-12 abortions in her lifetime. According to the Russians we spoke with, men were not a steady influence; at least 50 percent – some estimate 70-90 percent – were alcoholics.

Human lives mean nothing under communism. St. Petersburg, a beautiful city, has the breathtaking church of St. Isaac's, which stands on 100,000 graves of the men who built it. Some towns have no names. What we saw, heard, and experienced kept us going back. We just couldn't stop. Signs that read, "There is no God, you have no soul" hung above all Russian school doors. However, our dependable God encouraged us with daily miracles; it was wonderful to watch the Lord at work.

Some of my most rewarding ministry was with Pete and Judy Woznick, Maury Graham, Jim and Kay Acheson, John McLaughlin, and Velma as we taught business ethics classes called *Dialogue in Christian Ethics*. It was stressful because going in since we didn't know who we would be talking to. Would we be teaching farmers or metal workers or attorneys? Pete spoke Russian but didn't use it, so in our free time Pete listened to learn who we were working with and what their needs were, and Velma wrote in shorthand what Pete heard. At night, we would adjust our next day's curriculum to the class in front of us. We found new friends and worked in many incredible events like the business seminars, seminars on Christian ethics and morality, leading a work team, etc. – whatever it was they needed to know, we joyfully provided.

Wayne Wingfield from North Carolina, one of our team members, sent us an interesting report about School #35 once he returned home:

> *Monday evening was the opening of Teacher's Conference in Vladimir, Russia. All 29 who went to help with the CoMission short-term seminar were instructed to mingle with the teachers in the foyer before the session began in the auditorium. I spoke with a dozen or so of the 150 teachers who attended the first session; there were two teachers and a principal to whom I felt especially drawn. As we filed in for the opening session in the auditorium, I sat with these three.*
>
> *Wednesday evening was our second Teachers' Conference, and as we again greeted the teachers in foyer, I met about a dozen of them. The two teachers from Monday night insisted I sit with them, and I noticed they were carefully taking notes on everything shared by the leader. Nina outlined her notes while Valentina was writing every word shared by the speaker.*
>
> *Near the end of the session, Nina wrote a personal note to me: "Come to School #35. Welcome, tomorrow." I explained I had no control over the assignments but assured her someone would come to their school soon. I did not have an interpreter when I spoke with them, and I was not sure they understood me.*

We concluded with devotions after each evening's activities, and before going to bed were given our assignments for the following day. The instructions included the schools to which we were assigned and a list of the members of our team. Written on my assignment sheet was "School #35." I was amazed – I hadn't told anyone of the note I had received!

After lunch on Thursday, I couldn't wait to arrive at School #35. Nina, along with some other teachers, greeted us with big smiles at the front of the school as if to say, "I knew you were coming to my school today."

Nina escorted us to the biology lab, which was filled with juniors and seniors. This was Nina's biology class, which included evolution charts all along one wall. After introductions, I gave a 15-minute message on "One." I shared with the class and teachers basic biblical truths, all inspired by the Holy Spirit. I related that there is:

1. *One people*
2. *One book, the Bible*
3. *One Creator*
4. *One Savior*

Following my brief message to the class, the students asked questions of our panel of CoMission representatives. The session lasted more than two hours and when it ended, I went to the door to greet students as they left.

Nina insisted that my translator and I follow her into the hall. She took us to the opposite side of the large school building and down one floor. I wasn't sure where we were going, but when she opened a classroom door, Valentina was there. She welcomed my translator and me into her class of third-grade boys and girls. As I entered the room, the whole class stood together at attention until Valentina said, "You may take your seats, students."

Then Valentina told me, "My students have prepared something for you."

I listened as they recited something in Russian for me. When they were finished, I asked my translator to have Valentina explain what they had recited. I was amazed when she replied, "That was John 3:16-17." The children had hidden these words in their hearts: "For God so loved the world, that He gave His only Son, so that everyone who believes in Him will not perish, but have eternal life. For God did not send the Son into the world to judge the world, but so that the world might be saved through Him."

After congratulating the students and teacher, I asked her how many verses they had memorized. Valentina said she was not exactly sure, but many. Then she showed me a notebook containing all the verses they had memorized, I'm sure there were 50 or more. I asked her if she had been teaching the students the verses all year and Valentina responded, "Oh no, just since the CoMission commissioning service in November. (This incident happened only three months later, in February). It was at that service I received my first Bible." I asked her how long she had been a Christian, and again she replied, "Since November at the CoMission commissioning services."

Praise God for CoMission! Many Russians will never be the same. Neither will their nation nor short-term CoMission seminar leaders like me. And yes, School #35 will never be the same.

Thank you for your part in sending me as your representative to a beautiful country with beautiful people.

-Wayne

Velma and I were excited to be a part of the CoMission. J.B. Crouse, president of OMS International, was a bundle of nonstop energy, a continual fire for God and His Kingdom. All of us tasted and experienced God's Spirit drawing us together. We couldn't stop talking about what God was doing in the former Soviet Union.

Our friend, Iris Riggs, was sitting with Velma and me at a social event, and she asked, "Why is it that everyone who has been to Russia cannot stop talking about it?"

An hour later we stopped telling her when the event ended, but we could have gone on much longer. We couldn't stop talking about it! And we were not alone: of the 225 people we took to Russia, every single one fell in love with the Russian people.

The 12 leaders of CoMission have written a book called *The CoMission.* Here are excerpts from pages 33 and 46:

> In 1997, when the CoMission officially ended, there were no assets to distribute. The 60-plus million dollars that was raised and invested through the scores of established ministry organizations that comprised its membership nearly all found its way into ministry right on the field – not in corporate overhead." Pg. 33
>
> From the beginning to Russia, we envisioned the convocation strategy as taking advantage of "a window of opportunity," one that we thought might not last more than five years. From May 1991 (the first convocation) to December 1996 (the last), 136 convocations were completed in 116 different cities. They drew a total of 41,618 educators ... So great was the educators' interest in knowing more about this God who loved them and died for them, that our short-term volunteer teams were overwhelmed." Pg. 46

Of those 225 people who traveled to Russia with me, more than 26 percent of them became engaged in ministry in a new way, joining in the ministry in Russia or answering God's call to full-time service wherever else He led them.

Over the 12 trips I've made to Russia in my lifetime, God gradually dissipated my cynicism as I saw the people and felt their pain.

God used the Russian people to change my heart and the hearts of my traveling companions as we ate, prayed, and lived a little bit of their difficult lives with them. We visited homes in frigid weather with no heat and saw ladies performing extreme manual labor.

Yet after shaking hundreds of rough, chapped hands, being hugged by countless believers who thanked us over and over for being there for them, I found that my eyes kept sweating. I learned that it is hard to be cynical when looking at folks through heartfelt tears.

**See the Glossary for a description of CoMission.*

Freedom in the Dark

Unnamed Communist Leader

"But know that the Lord has set apart the godly man for Himself; the Lord hears when I call to Him" (Psalm 4:3).

As a part of our traveling in the 1990s, we met an internationally known, highly educated Communist leader who held a position of great demand and extreme pressure. Nevertheless, he graciously accepted a Bible from one of our fellow workers who was brave enough to offer it to him. He was extremely interested in finding out what was in this forbidden book, so in his flat he pulled up boards in the floor under his bed and secretly hid his Bible there.

His daily routine did not allow him to return to his home until late in the day. Before he retired for the evening, he would go into his bedroom and pull down the window shades. He carefully removed the boards under his bed, took the Bible, and crawled into bed with a flashlight. With the windows covered and blankets over the top of him, he began to read the Word of God in secret.

While he was reading one evening, the Lord brought salvation to him. Not many know of this great leader's faith in Christ because if it became public knowledge, death would be his certain reward. Therefore, he discreetly moves about the world with a guarded ability to share his faith in Christ. This Communist leader wants to share his faith, but he cannot. Most of us have the freedom to share our faith in Jesus, but we seldom do.

We recently learned our Communist friend has more freedom to share his faith and takes the privilege to disciple others. He is under the grace and protection of our Lord.

Let us remember the words of Jesus: "As you sent Me into the world, I also have sent them into the world" (John 17:18), because you can never assume to know who's eager to partner with Jesus.

Sell Cows, Save Souls

Rich Ring

Introduction by Warren Hardig

Pennsylvania dairy farmer Rich Ring, after a lot of persuasion and prayer, sold some of his cows and went to Russia to teach *Christian Ethics and Morality from a Biblical Perspective*. Rich kept his heifers, intending to come back and quickly start production. However, after a few days ministering in the north of Russia he wrote home and said, "Sell the heifers!"

When I asked a Russian man years ago, "Have you accepted Jesus?" he replied, "I am watching you to see who He is." I quickly said a prayer, asking the Lord to let him see the kindness of the MFM men around him, knowing, "What is desirable in a man is his kindness" (Proverbs 19:22). Certainly there were other Russians watching Rich when he was there.

What amazes me is that God calls each of us to serve Him in whatever capacity we are willing and able to do. You can serve as a missionary in any country of the world through prayer.

Not many people know of the service to the Lord folks like Rich have carried out, but our God does. Their selflessness in giving their time, talents, and treasures is immeasurable.

Where are the great men? They are everywhere, and we have to find them. I have met them in offices, cotton fields, fishing boats, and at construction sites. When you meet them for the first time, most likely, some of the first words out of their mouths will be, "I am just an ordinary guy."

"For the eyes of the Lord move to and fro throughout the earth that He may strongly support those whose heart is completely His" (2 Chronicles 16:9).

Here is a small segment from Rich for your encouragement.

I had been a dairy farmer all my life and believed home was the place to be. My mother told me I was so shy that I cried for six weeks when I started school. At 16, I accepted Jesus Christ as my Savior. I went on to marry a Christian girl. We both wanted to serve God in some capacity, and expected to do that at home in our church and neighborhood.

In November 1970, we were challenged to visit the mission field. God didn't leave us alone. He performed a miracle, and, in February 1971, we found ourselves in Colombia, South America. After returning to Colombia several more times on short witness and work crusades, we had a desire to do something more long term. We applied to the mission board, but due to lack of further education and experience, we were told there wasn't a need for us.

I involved myself in Men for Missions, began a local council and, as the MFM mission statement says, encouraged many to *Do, Go, and Give whatever God asks*.

When we first heard about CoMission* and the cry from the Russian Department of Education for the Christians from America to "come help us teach Christian morals and ethics to our children," we were pricked in our hearts, yet we didn't think that we would qualify. We weren't educators. But after praying for two years and trying to recruit others, we learned that to qualify for this particular mission, we simply had to be able to "push a button, hug a child, and pray with a friend." We could certainly do that, so we applied and were accepted. As we watched God bring in the necessary funds, we knew He was leading us to go. We sold all our cows, and in January 1996, we were in Rybinsk, Russia, for one year.

I dare say it was the richest year of our lives. We knew our prayer supporters at home were faithful and God's Spirit was alive in our midst. We watched as God drew many souls to Himself. We clung to His promise in John 12:32: "When I am lifted up from the earth, I will draw all men to Myself."

We shared the Gospel with people in the market, on the train, and in our apartment building. People were looking for a God who, they were told, didn't exist. We eventually began five Bible studies, including two in schools and two in our neighborhood. They continue to meet weekly, led by Russian Christians.

**See the Glossary for a description of CoMission.*

Sharp Sword

Loren Minnix

Introduction by Warren Hardig

A great man is comfortable telling others how Jesus forgave him and made a difference in his life. He is not ashamed to ask others to become believers. He has been known to leave the comforts of his home and go far away to another country to share God's love, only to discover through his experience that his prior ambitions were not as important as he thought. Loren Minnix is such a man. Here is a small segment of his story …

I have served on the MFM board and eventually became president of the American Cabinet of MFM. After I served my time, my brother, John Minnix, became a board member. He told me about a book R. Gene Bertolet was writing titled *Spiritual Warfare*. Gene had made a powerful presentation at a MFM conference in Waco, Texas, and John was anxious to tell me about it when he got home.

John and I both served in the military – John, a Navy Seabee and I, a Marine. He knew how pugilistic I was by nature, I always loved a good fight! And he also knew how much I changed after I gave my heart to Jesus Christ, who softened my heart for His Word, His people, and His cause. He also hardened my heart against evil and the tactics of Satan. To me, sin became exceedingly wicked. The closer I drew to God and His Word, the greater my love for Him grew. Sin and evil became more obvious and horrible to me, and my heart's desire was to combat it any way I could. Thy Word, oh God … Thy Word!

During my four-year tour in the Marines, I was exposed to a lot of rottenness in this world, so I wasn't surprised by much of what I saw and experienced when visiting different countries and cultures through missions. My converted eyes, however, saw more clearly how sin holds its victims in bondage. I grieved over this deeply. And I literally wanted to combat it.

While others were spending time talking about the love of God, I felt I could prove my love for Him by hating the things He hated. "The fear of the Lord is to hate evil; pride and arrogance and the evil way and the perverted mouth, I hate" (Proverbs 8:13).

Therefore, I was ripe for a battle against evil when I read *Spiritual Warfare: Tactical and Strategic Intercession through the Holy Spirit of God* by Gene Bertolet. God fights His battles through us, as we allow Him to lead us into the labyrinths of a desperate world.

For protection, wherever we went in Haiti, we carried with us the spiritual weapons of war: Bibles and Gospel literature. No weapon ever formed is stronger than the Word of God: it is "living and active and sharper than any two-edged sword, and piercing as far as the division of soul and spirit, of both joints and marrow, and able to judge the thoughts and intentions of the heart" (Hebrews 4:12). Thy Word, oh Lord … Thy Word!

MFM put together and sent out teams of prayer warriors to tour troubled areas of Haiti, where prayer was needed and conducted. My team went to Sector Four and was led by Warren Hardig, at that time Executive Director of Men for Missions. Other team members were

Howard Young, Dick McLeish, and Harold Floyd, plus Emanuel Felix from Haiti, who joined us as interpreter and evangelist.

In Sector Four, a notorious prison was located in the town of Gonaives, Haiti. I have visited county jails and state prisons in the U.S., but I have never seen anything as crude and antiquated as that prison. From the outside it looked like a huge stone castle with moss and tangled vines clinging to its walls. When the guards opened the ancient gates to allow us entry into the large interior courtyard, we were met with overwhelming sights and smells that sickened us.

A spirit of evil and desperation hung in the air. An adverse spiritual presence was so thick you could almost, as the old saying goes, "cut it with a knife." It was as obvious as the huge stone walls that surrounded us. In spite of all that, I sensed the peaceful presence of the Lord with us.

We were locked inside the prison yard and surrounded by barred cells full of prisoners. Cells built to house four inmates were overcrowded with up to eight inmates. It was extremely hot, and the prisoners were stripped to their shorts.

The MFM team went from cell to cell and let the prisoners look us over to ease their curiosity. We prayed silently for Emanuel Felix as he presented the Gospel and gave literature to each inmate. He introduced the team as caring Christian Americans who had come to visit them and to pray. Thy Word, oh God … Thy Word!

All of a sudden, a disturbance arose from somewhere in the prison; we were told we had to get out immediately. As we were hurried toward the gates, one of the prisoners yelled at us, "I need to talk to you!"

In broken English he quickly told me how and why he was in prison, and he didn't know what to do. While Emmanuel was hastily translating, I shared my testimony and the glorious Gospel with this inmate. I told him he needed to pray and accept Christ into his heart and life.

The guards were yelling for us to hurry! I knew I would have to condense my delivery into a minute or less, and allow time for translation, and then prayer. After my testimony, the prisoner disappeared back into the dark recesses of the cell and reappeared wearing a white shirt. He knelt down on his side of the bars and reached his arms through the bars for a personal touch during prayer.

Warren Hardig stepped forward, knelt down, took the prisoner's hands, and began to pray for him. The rest of the team gathered around, laying hands on Warren to support him as he did battle for God in enemy territory. He prayed the inmate through to victory while Emmanuel simultaneously translated.

The guards continued to push us to get out of there. We left a new saint of God rejoicing as we quickly departed sooner than we had planned.

It all happened faster than I can write about it. But it was so real and powerful that years later it still remains an unbelievably vivid memory. My prayer is that lives were changed for the glory of God and that the seed planted there still thrives. I couldn't help but think of a twist on the old saying, "Fools for Christ rushed in where angels feared to tread." Thy Word, oh God! Thy Word!

A spiritual battle was fought that day. In the brightness of a stifling hot, sunny day, we entered into a miserable black atmosphere and a new light was born in another human heart. God was in charge as mighty men of valor stepped into the spiritual fray and wrested another sinful wretch, just like we had been, from the gloom.

As we were rushed out of the prison, we could only pray that the light of a new saint would pervade that darkness and multiply among the men there. I wonder: If I were to hear that man's testimony today, what it would be?

Thy Word, oh God … Thy Word!

Praying for Others Anywhere

Warren Hardig

Haiti, the poorest country in the Western Hemisphere, has been used by God to challenge many North American visitors to evaluate their priorities and life ambitions. On one of my many trips to Haiti, God challenged my presumptions.

On this visit, a group of us were with a church near the border of the Dominican Republic to do evangelism. Each morning our team loaded into the OMS van with two Haitian ladies who purchased food *en route* to our ministry site, usually two or three live chickens which they would butcher and prepare over a charcoal fire for the evening meal.

Our worship center was a large tree with a gas lantern hanging from a lower branch to illuminate the area. Bamboo poles sticking up a few inches off the ground holding 8' poles made crude, uncomfortable benches. Some folks sat on the ground, but the bamboo poles were the best choice for seating. Each person on our MFM team had a Bible, a supply of invitations and some tracts. Don't ask me to explain how you invite someone to a meeting under a tree, but it works there!

We also had an interpreter to guide us, enabling us to communicate with the residents surrounding our center of activity. Creole was the language of our target audience.

Walking to my assigned area meant going down a trail similar to what our livestock carved back on the farm. A large tree stood at the one junction in the trail, giving sweet relief from the burning sun.

Most mornings, a witch doctor was stationed at this particular junction, and I found myself walking off the trail to avoid a confrontation with him. On our last evening, my interpreter and I were at that intersection by the big tree. On a chair leaning against the tree was a lady with a filthy bandage wrapped around her left leg just below the knee. Infected blood was oozing out of her leg above and below the bandage. As we approached her, I handed her an invitation to church that evening and a Gospel tract.

Her response was to inform me that her leg hurt. I replied something to the effect, "Jesus can help you."

"But my leg hurts," she said.

"Jesus can help you," I said. We continued these simple phrases back and forth several more times, like we were playing a game of table tennis.

Then the clear voice of God spoke in my ear, "Am I who you have been saying I am?"

In that moment I realized I was being a religious politician. I could pray in a Methodist or a Baptist church, and I could pray in a Presbyterian church. But when I heard His question, I responded in my heart, "Yes, you are, Lord!"

I reached out my right hand and placed it on the lady's shoulder, raised my left hand to God, and began praying a prayer aloud that would have made any Pentecostal proud. I asked for Jesus to touch and heal her. I prayed with focused intensity, asking our wonderful God to meet her every need, trusting His love and provision for her.

After a few minutes of prayer, we left the lady and went to the dinner prepared by our Haitian friends. Then our team went to the evening service, where we dutifully sat on the bamboo poles without groaning. After three or four songs, the lady with the bad leg came into the light and sat in front of and a little to the right of me.

The service continued for another hour, all of us on the team suffering paralysis in our backsides from sitting on the bamboo poles. I managed to get up and take a few steps to thank our lady with the bad leg for coming.

"My leg is better," she said, then disappeared into the dark.

I don't know what happened in her body or her heart. All I know is that God helped her … and He helped me, too. In my heart and soul, I was reminded that it is not enough to be religious. I need to be more like Christ. I need to trust Him and be bold for Him, praying for others even in situations where I am not comfortable. I need to pray for others, whether it is in a crowded bus station or in a quiet place on a lonely hill.

"The name of the Lord is a strong tower; the righteous run into it and is safe" (Proverbs 18:10).

Missionary Without a Portfolio

Koy Bryant

Introduction by Warren Hardig

The life and experiences of heating and air conditioning man Koy Bryant provide strong proof of the truth of Proverbs 19:8: "He who gets wisdom loves his own soul; he who keeps understanding will find good."

Koy demonstrates a willingness to serve and is available for whatever God asks. His innumerable loving acts of service include:

- helping to deliver a baby in Ecuador;
- fixing a new clothes dryer by using a syringe from the medical clinic in Ecuador;
- building cabinets in Spain after pouring a concrete floor;
- erecting a cross on a church in Estonia with the help of a Communist friend from Russia and an Estonian friend;
- leading several work teams to Mexico;
- building a playground for school children;
- installing heating and air conditioning in a Russian seminary; and
- installing a huge air conditioning unit in a mega church in Manila, Philippines.

It is easy to see how Proverbs 19:8 rings true in his life. You have to wonder where such talent comes from. We can also apply, "He who gives attention to the word will find good, and blessed is he who trusts in the Lord" (Proverbs 16:20).

Koy has many friends all over the world who benefit from his multiple skills, yet I believe most, if not all, would say that what they love most is his heart! Read on, and see if you can see …

I stood near a precipice on a dark, foggy night, high in the Andes Mountains of Ecuador, holding a flashlight in one hand and a stick in the other. The only other light visible on the narrow passage came from the headlights of a truck backing toward the precipice. The rule in these treacherous mountains dictates that the vehicle with the right of way stays close to the mountain while the other vehicle must stop and back up as close as possible to the edge of the precipice to allow for passage.

I was a stranger in this part of the world, having arrived in Ecuador the day before. As I tried helping my new friend in the truck, using the stick to find the edge of the precipice, I couldn't help thinking, *Lord, how did I get here on this fog-enshrouded mountain so far from home?*

The answer to that question lies in my life story.

Divinely Ordained Roots

No man is an island, and to know me is to know my grandfather, Jacob Fleck. He was the child of German immigrants, and his family settled in southern Illinois in the late 1800s. Grandpa, like his father and brothers, was a farmer.

As a young man, Grandpa, his wife, and their young children attended a Methodist church where he was saved. Later he attended a Holiness Camp meeting* several miles from their home. At one of these meetings he testified to being sanctified, meaning surrendering your life to God, expecting His Holy Spirit to develop your spiritual formation.

Grandpa farmed several acres of ground. Not long after his experience of sanctification he told his wife he believed God wanted him to start a camp meeting. He said he was going to purchase 20 shady acres in southern Illinois on which to build an outdoor tabernacle with room for cottages to accommodate the campers.

The tabernacle went up and the first Jacob's Camp Meeting was held in 1910. Those 10-day meetings continued for more than 90 years. My mother, Lana, was Jacob's daughter. Her husband, Bill Bryant, was a farmer; they had six children and I was the youngest of the bunch. I grew up attending the camp meetings every year, hearing many great preachers, and enjoying great singing by the song leaders who were a part of the evangelistic team.

One of those singing evangelists was J. Byron Crouse. He and his family came several times to the camp meetings and enjoyed meals in my folks' home.

During those times the Crouses' son J.B. and I became friends. Neither of us ever suspected that one day our paths would cross again when J.B. was president of OMS International.

Life-Changing Introductions

In 1963, I married Margaret Wicker and introduced her to Jacob's Camp. We didn't know then what a profound influence that sacred place would have on our family, nor how it would be God's avenue for discovering His will for our lives. There our older son, Eric, walked the aisle and gave his young heart to Jesus.

One day of each 10-day camp was designated Missionary Day, when missionaries on home assignment from either OMS International or World Gospel Mission would share stories of their lives in their particular field of service.

At that time I worked as the mechanical maintenance person for a nursing home corporation, where the owners recognized my skills and entrusted me with the mechanics of two nursing homes. I also supervised and built residential homes and an apartment building for them. It was God's school of training.

My heart was touched with the challenges the missionaries faced on foreign fields. I listened as they shared how often they needed to deal with some of the everyday problems of living abroad where there was no one to fix the heat, the stove, plumbing, etc. that invariably broke down. Some were even responsible for building projects where they felt unqualified.

These men had been called to preach and minister. I thought, *Couldn't God also call someone to go and help them fulfill their calling?* I shared with Margaret what was taking shape in my mind and heart, and we began to pray how God could, in some way, use us on a mission field. We were young and willing to go anywhere He sent us. But where and how?

In the 1960s, sending laymen to the mission field was a novel idea. MFM was in its infancy and we had never heard of it. But we believed if we did our part the Lord would open the door. Our first step was to apply through our church mission board. We received a very polite letter telling us unless we had college or seminary training, we would not qualify. Next, we applied to an interdenominational mission society and received the same polite answer.

Not sure what else to do, we left it in God's hands.

God's Timing

A few years passed and we still had not heard from the Lord about mission work. I did, however, become president of the board of Jacob's Camp, which became the avenue God used to open His door to mission fields ahead. There we met Dr. John Logan, who came to the camp as an evangelist. He became our spiritual father and mentor. Dr. Logan, a Scottish preacher, had been president of several Bible colleges. Oswald Chambers had previously been president of one of those colleges, as well as another college in the United States. Dr. Logan served as chaplain to the King of England and knew the future Queen Elizabeth as a young girl.

For some reason known only to God, Dr. Logan took a liking to us and our young sons, Eric and Neil. God's ways are so full of pleasant surprises, are they not?

Over the years, Dr. Logan became a fixture in our home. As a consequence of his sermons at the camp, he was often called to preach in churches near us and in neighboring Indiana. When he stayed with us, we would invite others for Bible study and worship, because our home had become a house church. Dr. Logan knew about our love for missions and our desire to find a place of service.

Through Dr. Logan we met Bill and Joyce Oden. Bill pastored a Wesleyan church in Evansville, Indiana, and at that time in their lives they were feeling a call to full-time missionary service. Through contacts with OMS International, Joyce invited Valetta Steel to come to her home for a ladies' mission day, and Joyce asked my wife to attend.

As Margaret listened to Valetta share her life story, she was gripped with a yearning to find God's place for us somewhere on a mission field.

Dr. Logan visited us soon after and told us he would be preaching at a church in Indianapolis. He asked us to come and told us he would make arrangements for us to meet Dr. Wesley Duewel, president of OMS, who he thought could perhaps give us some direction. We met with Dr. Duewel, who told us about MFM and its use of laymen on the mission field. That was our open door, although we didn't realize how big that door would be.

That day we filled out an application to go on the next mission trip, a witness crusade to Haiti. We also learned there was to be an MFM retreat in Albion, Illinois, a town not far from us. We eagerly attended that meeting and met Warren Hardig, MFM's Central Regional field director. Little did we know what a bond of fellowship and love would be forged with Warren and his wife, Velma. We had no idea of the 35-plus years of Thanksgiving dinners and exciting quail hunts awaiting us with this couple!

When we told church friends we would be going to Haiti, to our surprise another couple came to us and asked if we thought they, too, could come on the trip. They applied and were able to go as well. We so anticipated our first missionary excursion!

The First of Many Journeys

Since the trip was scheduled to be a witnessing crusade, not a work mission, we visited several churches in Haiti and gave our testimonies. Then one day we walked five miles uphill to a village, and I ended up putting a tin roof on a church. I also got to help the nurse in the mobile medical clinic we took with us. There I saw a baby who was dying of typhus and could not be helped. I was crushed.

We had attended an OMS convention where I met Simon Avila and his wife, Cecilia, Mexican singing evangelists who ministered at the convention. I decided to go to Mexico with Simon, who returned to his hometown several times a year to hold revival services. He had asked me if I would come and help build a new church in his village, which had no Protestant church.

Our teenage son Eric, along with another young man in our church, went with me to help. When they came back, they shared their experience with our church. As a result, two other young men in the church told me if I went again, they wanted to go, too! A few months later those two young men and I returned to complete the work on the church.

During the time we had a house church, I became friends with L.M. Huff, the Baptist preacher in our town, and we began to meet weekly for prayer and Bible study. I asked him to disciple me. He was uncertain how to do that, so we learned together. We joined that church and have been members for more than 40 years now.

When we first met L.M., he was interested to learn that we worshiped in our home and placed great importance on missions. He wanted to lead his church into a personal involvement by going to a foreign mission field. The two young men who went with me to Simon's village in Mexico were members of his church. They returned home excited and, eager to share their experience with the church, told how they had been able to work on the mission. That began a buzz in the church because these were laymen, not preachers or teachers, and they were changed by their experiences. People began talking about the potential of going on a missions trip, not just giving a donation for missions work.

Ecuador Deliveries

In 1976, MFM asked me whether I could go to Ecuador and install plumbing in the annex of the hospital/clinic in Saraguro. Dr. Bill Douce and his wife Eilene, along with Bruce and Mabel Callender, were the missionaries there.

Now you know why I was on that fog-shrouded mountain road in Ecuador – it was Bruce Callender backing that truck up toward the precipice. He and I had gone to Cuenca for some needed plumbing supplies and were on the road back to Saraguro.

I have often said, "When you go to the mission field to do one job, you will often find that God has other unexpected projects for you." It was Ecuador that first taught me this. Soon after I arrived, Dr. Douce and his wife had to leave Saraguro for several days. The day he was to leave, an elderly man came to the hospital. He was almost blind from cataracts and asked the doctor if he could help him see again. Dr. Douce said he could do the surgery, but advised the man he would be unable to return home for 10 days. The man said he was willing to stay.

Dr. Douce asked me if I would take care of the man for those days, because his eyes would be bandaged the entire time. I fed him, took him to the bathroom, and did whatever needed doing. I came to love this old man and prayed each day for his healing and that he would know the love of the Lord through the work of the missionaries. I wanted to share God's love as well, and I returned home minus the shoes and clothes I gave him.

When the bandages were removed, everyone rejoiced with the man who was able to see again. Dr. Douce gave him a pair of glasses donated by people in the United States.

While the doctor was gone, some men brought in a woman who was in labor. Mabel Callender, the nurse on duty at the clinic, asked me to assist her with the delivery! I, a farm boy who had delivered many animals and was always up for a challenge, said, "Of course I will help!"

I had the privilege of catching the baby as he entered this world, cleaning and wrapping him in swaddling clothes and putting a tiny cap on his head, a custom for newborns in Ecuador. The husband and other men returned later that evening and took the mother and baby home, three mountains away.

One last project remained before I left for home. The Douces had been given a clothes dryer by someone in the States, which arrived in Ecuador while I was there. They were so excited to receive it because it rains every afternoon in the mountains and drying clothes is difficult. When they unpacked it, though, they discovered it was configured for natural gas and the only energy source available was liquid petroleum gas (called "LP"). That was a great disappointment! I looked it over and asked Dr. Douce to show me all his needles. I carefully inspected them and found just the one I thought would make a suitable LP gas opening. I broke the needle off and put the base into the opening and – *voila!* – they had a dryer that could be used in Ecuador!

As I flew home, I realized I had accomplished a plumbing job and more! God was using me just as I had sensed several years ago. Even without my having a college or seminary degree, He had a place for me. As I said a prayer of thanks on that flight, I wondered, *Where will God take me next?*

Needed Right on Time

About an hour and a half outside Madrid, Spain, OMS maintains a campground facility. In 1977, the work there was just beginning. They started with a building they used as a dormitory but were in the process of building a larger place.

MFM was informed they very much needed a plumber. Margaret and I and fellow MFMer Charlie Smith, who along with his wife Marie and their two sons, Barry and Dennis, found ourselves sitting in a New York airport, waiting to board a flight to Madrid. We men would be working on plumbing, while our wives would cook for the team. Missionary John Turnidge met us at the airport, and one of his first questions was, "What have you come to do?"

Somewhat surprised at his inquiry, I answered, "We have come to put the plumbing in the new camp building."

How very well we remember John's answer: "The last thing we need is a plumber!"

We were all shocked because of the original request we received for a plumber. Everyone else was disappointed, but I said, "We *are* going to put the plumbing in."

I had come to do plumbing, and plumbing I would do! After checking the building, I learned John was right: it was not ready for plumbing. After a few days of work, though, the building was ready.

Before we left, we helped a carpenter install kitchen cabinets and poured concrete for a floor. John was very glad the plumbing was done!

Divine Connections

God's Spirit was reviving our home church through the missionary vision He had given our pastor. Even those who did not go to a field were excited about what was happening, and many supported the work through their donations.

Pastor L.M. had a vision and kept asking the Lord to show him how to fulfill it. The answer wasn't long in coming. In 1980, L.M. attended an alumni seminary reunion at Bolivar Missouri Baptist

College, which reunited him with one of his seminary friends, Olan Runnels, the Director of Missions at the college. Olan was leading a team of college students to Mexico that summer to build some Bible schools and asked L.M. if his church would be interested in doing some needed construction work. L.M. told Olan about me and my involvement with Men for Missions and about those who had gone on church trips.

It was planned that Olan and I would go to Mexico to meet with Van Gladen, the Baptist missionary in Mexico. We toured several villages where Van knew there were needs, met with the Mexican pastors of churches, and came home with a three-week plan that Olan presented to our church. The response was overwhelming: 35 people volunteered to go for part or all of the three weeks! They were eventually joined by three more couples, two from Baptist churches and one from a Methodist church. These couples went on many of the Mexico mission trips our church made in the following years.

I led our church's yearly Mexico mission trips until 2004, when our missionary deemed them too unsafe to continue. Our work in the later years had been over the border in Nueva Laredo, where we worked on churches, pastors' homes, and orphanages; we went wherever Van Gladen and later Dr. Elizeo Vega determined our work was needed. We worked with our hands, shared our testimony of God's grace in churches and with the unsaved, and worshiped with our Mexican Christian brothers and sisters.

Domestic Projects

Along with our work on the mission field, we also tackled projects at the OMS/MFM headquarters in Indiana. In 1979 and 1980, our local MFM council worked at OMS on a duplex being built for OMS staff. In 1981, we refurbished the MFM office building. In 1991, Neil and I installed new boilers in the OMS administration building, and later that year installed a new air conditioning system. In 1994, Neil and I put a new air conditioning system in the MFM office, across the parking lot from the OMS main building.

Also in 1994, I led a team of 15 people from the church who went to Newton, Georgia, to help clean up a church devastated in the flooding caused by tropical storm Alberto. The congregation appreciated their newly cleaned church.

To Russia With Love

The fall of the Soviet Union in the early 1990s opened a door for Christian ministries. In 1996, I joined a work team led by Warren Hardig that went to Vladimir, Russia, to remodel a Christian cultural center OMS planned to use for meetings. Several men from our church who served on the MFM central regional council were on that team.

While there, I met Victor and his wife, Svetlana, who, along with Natasha, a young Russian woman, served as our interpreters. In the short time we were together we developed a close bond. Svetlana expressed she would like to visit the United States during Christmas, a wish that later developed into great significance for us.

When the job was finished in Vladimir, Warren and I with some others on the team flew to Estonia to survey the country. MFM had contacts in Estonia and wanted to send in a work team. We traveled to the small country located off the Baltic Sea. Through previous contacts we met a Baptist pastor in Parnu, who needed much work done on his church.

The people there had been ruled by Russia until they gained their independence after the breakup of the Soviet Union. After meeting with the pastor and assessing what could be done, we decided I would come back the following year to help the people work on the church.

Christmas Blessings

Returning from that trip, I was eager to share a plan I had devised on the way home. The plan, as it turned out, would have great impact on our family. I wanted to bring Victor and Svetlana to our house for Christmas! The plan was hatched in my mind when Svetlana said she would love to see Christmas in the United States.

We were eager to arrange their holiday visit. OMS had partnered with other Christian ministries in the CoMission, a program to teach Russian schoolteachers Christian ethics and morals so they could teach their students. Although Margaret had not yet met Svetlana, she had met Natasha, so she was excited at the prospect of having Russian guests at Christmas. And James Cutchin, a young man in our church, was glad our Russian friends were coming because he had been on the trip with me and knew them. He also helped contribute to the finances that helped them travel to the States.

They stayed with us for two weeks. What a blessed time it was! Both had become believers through the witness of OMS in Russia.

Christmas Eve was especially memorable as our family, along with our Russian guests, gathered around the Christmas tree to open presents. But before that, we read the Christmas story from the Bible, with Margaret reading in English and Victor in Russian. People from two countries, once enemies, now part of the same family, God's family, because of the miracle of His grace.

Return to a Beloved Land

In 1997, Margaret and I and another couple from our church, Doyce and Ruth Sheraden, went to Estonia to work at the Baptist church in Parnu. We stayed with the pastor's neighbors and ate many of our meals with members of the church. What wonderful, loving, and unforgettable Christians they were!

Because of the history between them, Estonians harbor enmity toward Russia. We did not realize this when we invited our Russian friends, Victor, Svetlana, Natasha, and her husband, Vladic, to come help us work on the church. They took the train from their home to Vladimir. Although our Estonian Christians were gracious, we were not sure how our hasty invitation would be received. We need not have been concerned, though. The Lord already had a plan: a Russian family in the church invited them to stay in their home!

Drawing All Men

On the last work day in Estonia, we had one final task that may have been the most important of all: raising the cross on the roof of the church. It took three men to lift it: one was Victor our Russian friend, the second was our Estonian brother, and I was the American. We each had hold of the cross as it was lifted high, and we worked together to attach it to the roof.

Jesus said, "And I, when I am lifted up from the earth, will draw all men to Myself" (John 12:32). Three nations, bitter enemies, were at the foot of the cross, brothers in Christ and part of the family of God – an amazing symbol of God's grace to us!

Later that same day we left for Tallinn, the ancient city and capital of Estonia, where we were to spend the weekend together before we flew home, and our Russian friends would take their train. That evening, sitting in the hotel and discussing our time at the church, our friends shared how much they enjoyed their visit with the Russian Christians. Vladic remarked how he had been impressed as he watched the three men from three nations put the cross on the church, something none of us will ever forget.

The Koy Bryant family.

Serving in the Philippines

I was asked to go to the Philippines, where OMS was building a large church in downtown Manila and wanted me to help install the air conditioning. I needed two men to accompany me and I prayed about who the Lord wanted them to be. Our son Neil, an air conditioning technician, and Phil Hoskins, a friend who attended the local Christian church, both volunteered and I was thankful for the Lord's provision for their long journey and for the incredibly challenging project. When we arrived it was still a three-story work in progress. Today, Faith Fellowship Church is a beautiful building in the heart of Manila whose attendance numbers in the thousands.

For me it was a wonderful reunion with some dear friends, because missionaries Bill and Joyce Oden and Ed and Rachel Erny were there. We had supported all of them for some time. We had known Bill and Joyce since he pastored the Wesleyan Church in Evansville, Indiana, and they had a special place in our lives.

Many Filipino workers lived in the church under construction rather than return home at night. They brought food to cook on make-shift stoves and slept on homemade bunks. The men on our team noticed that some of them seemed to be sick, lying on their bunks during the day. Our men also were amazed and sometimes fearful for the Filipinos as they worked three stories up, traversing the beams in their flip-flops and defying all rules of gravity with their fleet footedness.

Neil remembers how challenging the work was to install the air conditioning, but said he learned once more about persevering and working with what you had, as well as praying about every aspect of the work. The most important lesson learned was seeing God provide what we needed to do the job. It was amazing.

Neil and Koy Bryant.

Neil, Phil, Jim Acheson, and I all contracted dengue fever, a disease especially prevalent in the Philippines that is caused by a mosquito bite. The national workers who had been lying sick on their cots had dengue fever. I was especially sick, suffering a high fever as I traveled home – 14 hours on the plane and four more by car. However, all four of us soon recovered after being diagnosed by a doctor in Evansville who was from – of all places – Manila! God knows how to take care of His children. Later we learned Bill's case was so severe, he was put in the hospital for it. Thankfully, he too recovered.

In 2000, Neil and I went to Cap-Haitien to survey the air conditioning system at Radio 4VH prior to sending a work team. Later in the year we went back with Niece Edwards, a woman from our church, and some other MFMers.

That same year I went to Moscow and met with Dr. Alexei Bychkov, the president of the OMS seminary there. OMS wanted an assessment on an air conditioning system for the seminary. I met with Russian contractors about the materials and cost of installing the system and made some recommendations.

In October I went back to check out the system that had been installed. Margaret went with me and we had lunch in the seminary with many of the students. We learned that all of them rode the subway to school and were often accosted by hoodlums demanding their money as they left the subway because they knew they were seminary students.

It was our last trip to Russia, and we had the great opportunity to stay with Victor and Svetlana for several days in Vladimir. We spent a day in Moscow, sightseeing with Natasha and Vladic. It was a reunion to be treasured, much like being with our own children!

A Legacy of Service

A Christian's story is really God's story written through our lives. My story here began with my heritage through my grandfather, Jacob Fleck, and continues with my son Neil and grandson Reagan.

As a little boy, Neil always worked with me on my projects. I remember him at seven years old hammering nails into a shipping crate to send my motorcycle to a pastor in Haiti who needed it far more than I did.

As a teenager, Neil went with our church members on the Mexico mission trips and helped with whatever building project we were doing. He also attended the local Christian Church youth group, which was quite popular among the young people in the area. Their youth pastor, knowing about our church's mission trips, wanted to organize a youth mission trip in his church, so he asked me to come to their meeting and tell what it was like to take a mission trip, including how to organize one.

Neil, then 16, went with me and was asked by the pastor if he would go along to help lead the group. Going on that trip taught him a lot and empowered him from an early age. He said he knew what it felt like to be his dad, because he was the only one who had been to Mexico or on any mission trip and they kept asking him questions.

He told what he learned going to the mission field, especially how to persevere when things didn't go as planned, because they seldom did. But he shared that the other men and I never gave up or gave in; we prayed, and God always made a way. So Neil learned life skills, and learned to trust God as he watched us pray whenever we encountered a problem or difficult situation. He learned to pray for people as well as things, and saw God answer whatever need he and others encountered.

When Neil was in high school, he wanted to play football. When he tried out for the team, the coach told him it would require a total commitment of his time and asked him if he was willing to make that commitment. Neil told the coach he went on mission trips with his church, which would at times keep him from attending practice.

The coach said he would have to make a choice. Neil told me, "I didn't even have to think about it for a minute. I wasn't going to give up going on mission trips even if I wanted to be like my brother and play football."

Today Neil serves on the MFM Cabinet and has a very mission-oriented mentality. His heart has been especially drawn to Haiti, where he has worked at Radio Station 4VEH. He has taken his two teenaged sons, Reagan and Isaac, to Haiti, and plans to take his youngest son, Caleb, when the country is settled enough to allow them to go.

Reagan has recently come home from his second mission trip to Cuba. When he goes, he works with Filter of Hope, installing water filters in village homes to purify their water supply.

No believer's life story is specifically about the person, it is about God's story being written through that surrendered life. At the beginning of my life story, you may remember I did not have the necessary credentials to be a missionary. I had no educational degree then and I still don't. I had no portfolio. My prayer is that you may see in this story the grace of God and how He used an ordinary man like me to further the work of His Kingdom.

I like when God told Moses He had put his Holy Spirit in men He gifted to be craftsmen, uniquely capable of building the tabernacle in the wilderness (Exodus 31:3-5). Men just like the ones in this chapter, and the men in this entire book.

And perhaps … you.

**See the Glossary for a description of Holiness Camp meeting.*

Gate 29

Warren Hardig

Velma and I have been privileged to travel across the world and always enjoy hearing the Word of God preached wherever we are. One August morning in 2016 we were in Carmi, Illinois, to hear our friend Jim Slone preach at a nearby church. Velma woke up with poor balance that morning, however, and it has not left her. She describes it as trying to stand up in a kayak every day. This has changed our lifestyle and the amount of travel we are able to do.

We now limit our travel to North America, and even that is difficult for her to do. One trip in 2018 took us to Florida for our global Cabinet meetings. Our itinerary took us from Indianapolis to Charlotte to Orlando, with a four-hour layover in Charlotte. When we travel now, I keep several one-dollar bills in my pocket to tip wheelchair attendants who make it possible for Velma to navigate the airport much more quickly and easily. Upon our arrival in Charlotte we were met at the gateway door by Taylor, a kind gentleman with a wheelchair; the airlines had notified the gate attendants ahead of time.

"Are you Miss Velma?" he inquired.

"Yes," she said.

After she was comfortably seated in the wheelchair, we were taken up the concourse by our new friend who asked Velma if we should stop at the restroom.

While we waited, he asked what I did for a living. I told him I worked for a group called Men for Missions, and that we ask men to *Do whatever God asks of them, to Go wherever God asks them to go, and to Give whatever God asks them to give.* I told him we were a volunteer organization and we had just finished building 101 homes in Haiti for earthquake victims.

Our new friend, Taylor, said he would like to be a part of something like that. I promptly reached into my pocket and produced a business card for him, and we continued toward the center of the concourse. Taylor knew we had four hours before our next flight, so he asked us if we wanted to get something to eat. Having been through the Charlotte airport before, I knew they had excellent barbecue.

"Could I buy your lunch?" I asked. Surprisingly, he said yes.

Taylor was very attentive to Velma, so after we ordered our food, he said would get Miss Velma to a table right behind us, and help her get situated. I paid for our meal then took our tray of food to the table, sitting next to Velma and across from Taylor.

After I prayed for the meal, Taylor asked me, "Mr. Warren, how many countries have you been in?" I told him I had been privileged to touch ground in over 90 countries, but only ministered in about 46.

I proceeded to tell Taylor I only have one message: how Jesus forgave me of my sins.

I told him about growing up in southern Illinois and somehow convinced Velma to marry me, after meeting her at our local church. Taylor laughed and listened intently to every detail. I told him about my struggle with cigarettes and my desperate prayer to the Lord for deliverance. When I told him of the peace I found in Christ, I tapped his chest and asked him if he had that peace. He told me that he didn't have it but wanted it, so I told him we would find a quiet place to pray together.

We finished our meal and made the trip to our Gate 27, from which we would depart for Florida. Across the concourse was Gate 29, which I noticed was empty and dark, so we made our way there and our new friend Taylor asked Jesus for forgiveness and accepted Him into his heart. We went back to our departure gate and Taylor happily sat with us for as long as he could. He was terribly sad to leave our side, but he gave me his phone number and address before we boarded our plane so we could remain in contact.

We still call each other from time to time so I can pray for him. He always laughs with great joy and thanks me for praying. It was surely the best money I ever spent on a lunch. We will never forget Gate 29!

It Was a Great Ride, Wasn't It?

Jim Acheson

Introduction by Warren Hardig

Velma and I were privileged to have Jim and Kay Acheson on one of our first ministry teams to Russia. We soon found out that any project the Achesons committed themselves to was a commitment to see it completed, and completed with excellence. Our ministry teams in Russia took on a new flavor as we began dialogue and taught business ethics seminars. Jim and Kay were on board, and we all made new friends in the former Soviet Union.

You will read in Jim's testimony how he became the project manager for Radio 4VEH and Operation Saturation in Haiti. Jim and Kay worked tirelessly behind the scenes, averaging more than 50 hours a week. Their dedication to the project was a true labor of love. If you visited their home during Operation Saturation, you would see blueprints of the proposed broadcast center laid all throughout the house.

Kay worked on outfitting and decorating the kitchen for the new broadcast center. If that wasn't enough, Kay and Velma also worked on writing grants to help finance the project. This project was a hundred times larger than the average MFM project, and Kay, Velma, and I spent time visiting different foundations to pitch our ideas to garner their support. Our largest foundation request was $1 million; the smallest was $6,000. Our challenge to prospective donors was,

"Help us with the goal of reaching a million people in Haiti with the Gospel of Jesus Christ every day through Radio 4VEH." I am honored to have Jim share his story with us.

Jim, at our last U.S. MFM Cabinet meetings, challenged us by quoting his beloved Kay, "It was a great ride, wasn't it?"

Jim asked, "Are we just making memories, or are we leaving a legacy?" Here is his story …

I was born and raised on a farm during the Depression when farming was mostly done by hand and by horses. Threshing was done by equipment powered by big steam engines. We had no car, nor what others considered necessities. On occasion, we even used the farm tractor to get us to church.

My father was a workaholic and expected my brothers and me to follow his example. Even as a small lad, standing around or goofing off was not an option.

Later, when World War II started, my father got a job as a heavy equipment operator near Peru, Indiana, where they were constructing the Bunker Hill Naval Air Base (now Grissom Air Base). Once Bunker Hill was complete, my father went to Alaska as a bulldozer operator on a project constructing a pipeline through Canada and Alaska that would supply fuel to Alaskan military forces. Meanwhile, my mother, my two brothers, and I were left to handle the livestock and do all the farming.

When my father returned from Alaska, we bought a farm near Fort Recovery, Ohio. My father worked in the construction industry and was only home on weekends, so my brothers and I took care of the livestock and did the basic farming in his absence. Like many farmers, we had to rely on the few neighbors who owned combines or hay balers to do our harvesting. As the oldest son, my father had taught me how to write and use a checkbook to pay for the work. I was responsible for contacting the people who did the combining and hay baling and then paying them for their services. I was 12 years old.

Shortly after WWII, my father started his own heavy construction company. In 1948, he bought his first new Caterpillar bulldozer. Later on, I was taught how to operate it, and by the age of 16, I was a fairly accomplished dozer operator. My father was strict. If you got a bulldozer stuck by yourself, you had to get the bulldozer unstuck by yourself. At the end of the episode, his usual response was, "Did you learn anything?" That response has stayed on my mind and been applicable to all my life's experiences.

From a young age I was given many responsibilities in the business, and I was also involved in the local youth group. When I was growing up, folks in my church sent their kids to summer church camp for a week at Lakeside, Ohio, on Lake Erie. I wanted to go, but I had responsibilities. I told my father I was involved in the church youth group and had committed to take some of the kids to Lakeside Church Camp. It worked! It was on that trip I met a very special girl who later became my wife.

Shortly after I met Kay, we started dating. Being very shy, I figured I needed to impress her in a big way. So, when I picked her up one Sunday afternoon, I decided to show her a land-clearing project.

Suddenly, I had a brilliant idea: I would give my girl a ride on a bulldozer. So, I selected one of the bulldozers, a brand-new Caterpillar D-E (the largest two-seater built at that time). I helped Kay get up on the dozer and proceeded to start the pony engine and then the diesel engine. We were ready to go. I drove the dozer around for five or six minutes and then I spotted the ramp.

Suddenly, I had another "brilliant" idea: at full speed, we flew over the ramp where the dozer momentarily assumed a vertical position then miraculously teetered back and forth before landing back down on its tracks. We were engulfed in a cloud of dust. I was hanging on to the air cleaner and Kay was hanging on to the hood. We tumbled off the bulldozer. Our Sunday clothes were torn and covered with dust.

Well, mission accomplished. I had certainly impressed her. She looked at me and shook her head as she brushed herself off, smiled a little and muttered, "You're crazy! Next time, you can go by yourself!"

Later that summer we were in a serious head-on automobile accident, hit by some drunk teenagers. It wasn't pretty. Kay was seriously injured. I was lucky to walk away with only a few broken ribs and a damaged left arm. But Kay had facial injuries, a fractured skull, and the loss of sight in her right eye. For several weeks she laid in the hospital, where doctors performed surgery on her face and worked on saving her eye.

I was devastated! I prayed relentlessly for her recovery. With God's help, she survived.

We were married later that year, 1954. We soon began having children and building a family of our own.

I was still involved in the family construction business, which was growing as we undertook a variety of heavy construction projects throughout Indiana, Ohio, Michigan, and Illinois.

In the mid-1950s our company encountered problems on several of our road projects, especially on the Illinois Toll Road, later to become I-84. There were many delays due to legal right-of-way problems, causing financial problems for some companies. Unfortunately, ours was no exception. Also, since we were subcontractors on several projects, we were forced to accept delayed payments. Even relying on several of our other projects, we could not get solvent again.

Broke and with no decent job opportunities, I determined to get a college education, knowing no one could take that away from me. I knew I would have to work my way through college because we had no money, but in 1958, with a wife and four kids, I enrolled in college to earn a civil engineering degree.

During the summer months, I made good money using my skills in construction and highway work. After many challenges, I graduated from college in 1963 and went to work for a road and bridge contractor as an estimator and field engineer. But sometimes God speaks to us in strange ways to guide us in another direction.

One evening as I was working on I-74 as a field engineer, I noticed one of the grader operators staring at me. I made my way over to him.

"You having a problem?" I asked.

He looked at me and said, "Nope, but you are."

After that simple statement he tossed a quarter in my direction. When I caught it, I blurted out, "What's this for?"

He looked at me and said, "You went to college, didn't you? If I were you, I'd take that quarter, call the college, and get your money back."

I didn't call the college, but I did change jobs. Over the years, I spent time as an engineer for the city of Fort Wayne, worked for a consulting firm, and was a division supervisor for a major gas and electric utility company.

I retired from the utility company and began thinking. Over the course of my career, I had been involved in farming, engineering, construction, and marketing. *How could I use this experience to give back and serve others? What did God have in mind for me? What is life all about?* For me, it is about challenges and survival. Along the way, we seldom know how our actions and words will impact other people's lives, but our lives were certainly impacted by our daughter, Christine.

My involvement with MFM started because of Christine's connection with OMS. During college, Christine had gone to the Dominican Republic on a mission trip. On her trip back to Indiana, while in the Miami Airport, she was wondering and praying what God had in mind for her. A kind gentleman had sat down beside her and the two struck up a conversation about travel, missions, God's work, etc. That man's name was Wally Yoder. Wally told Christine about OMS and MFM and she was hooked. God's emissary, Wally Yoder, had answered her payers. Christine applied to OMS and was accepted. Her first assignment was Colombia.

Once Christine was settled there, Kay and I went to visit her. At that time an MFM work team was preparing to go to Colombia to do construction work and I was invited to go with the work team, so I accepted. Since I was already in Colombia visiting Christine, I met the team early the next morning, and we boarded a train packed with people, chickens, and various other objects. My comfort level, which had already taken a hit, was further diminished by seeing the bullet holes in the railway car we were riding in.

During our stay, we constructed small living quarters for a pastor and did other maintenance work on the compound, which was set up to teach vocational skills to the Colombians. I was extremely impressed by the dedication of the OMS personnel and the MFM volunteers and how they were able to minister to the Colombians.

A year later Kay and I were back in Colombia, traveling with Christine by airplane, bus, and boat to many villages and remote areas as she contacted needy pastors, schools, and families. It was an awakening for me. Here was my daughter, previously quite a non-adventurous bookworm, speaking Spanish and heading into remote areas of a foreign country to minister to the needs of the people there. I am always amazed how God works through dedicated people to spread the Gospel and help people in need.

In 1991, the Communist government of the Soviet Union ceased to exist as it had been and some of the former satellite countries and mother Russia opened up to the Western World, giving OMS and MFM a chance to have a presence in those countries. Being a history nut, I had an interest in knowing more about Russia; pairing that with my spiritual calling to get involved with OMS and MFM, I undertook a mission to share the Gospel with the Russian people. Given my mixed emotions about my possible involvement, I called Velma Hardig concerning the Russian program. Her enthusiasm for the project was contagious. Now I had to go!

Along with OMS and MFM people, Kay and I were soon on our way to Russia. What a change of pace: different customs, culture, rules, and a different language – one very difficult to comprehend. This trip was a great introduction to Russia and led to several future trips where we engaged in a variety of projects, such as encouraging small church startups, working with medical teams and school teachers, and conducting business seminars. Each trip and project was challenging, but rewarding and eye opening.

We learned the teachers hadn't been paid for months. The students, in addition to their studies, were responsible for some of the janitorial duties. Resources such as mops, paper, chalk, sports equipment, etc. were in short supply.

Time with the medical teams was interesting and productive. People came with all types of maladies and questions. We even had a couple of requests from folks about how to cure their dogs.

The way the business seminars came about happened unexpectedly. As we worked with the start-up church groups, we realized there were many women and children in attendance, but few men. So, we birthed the idea of having business seminars based on Christian principles, hoping that would draw out the men. A format was developed and our group, consisting of Pete and Judy Woznick, John McLaughlin, Maury Graham, Warren and Velma Hardig, and Kay and I presented seminars in cities in Russia, Estonia, etc.

The business seminars were a success and, as a result, several Russian businesses were birthed. When we presented a business plan, we would get two requests: "Teach us about marketing" and "tell us about ethics." In response to the latter, I remember Pete Woznick pulling out a dollar bill and pointing to the inscription: *In God We Trust*. Then he would explain how Christian values were important in starting and running a business. This illustration was remarkably effective in getting the message across to the attendees and afforded a good opening for a discussion on ethics.

Marketing was an interesting topic, as most were unfamiliar with the concept. We taught them that the bottom line was: even if you have the best product or service but no customers, your product or service is a dead commodity. It was an "Aha!" moment for many.

One precious memory of our Russian trips will forever be etched in my mind. We were attending a major religious service in a large Russian cultural center complex. On the walls were big pictures of Russian heroes, and the podium still featured a sizable emblem of the hammer and sickle. The place was packed with foreign missionaries, leaders, and Russian people. The service was meaningful and, as it ended, everyone started singing "How Great Thou Art" in seven or eight languages. With the vibrant singing of this great hymn ringing in my ears and the sight of the music directors from the hammer and sickle podium, one couldn't help getting choked up! God spoke to many of us that day. He truly works in many ways.

In addition to my mission trips to Russia, I had the opportunity to work on teams and mission trips to Ukraine, Estonia, the Philippines, Australia, New Zealand, Ecuador, Haiti, and Cuba, each significant in its own way.

One of the major MFM projects I was involved with was the design and construction of the new radio station for Radio 4VEH in Haiti. At a semiannual MFM meeting in 2001, we discussed building a new radio station to replace the old Radio 4VEH facility. During the discussion I needed to go to the restroom, and left. Upon my return, I discovered I had been appointed to be the engineer for the project! Little did I know the challenges that had to be addressed.

After analyzing the scope of the proposed project, it became apparent that the initial cost estimate was totally insufficient to fund such a huge project. We were going to have to rely on God's help to make this endeavor a reality. For starters, there were no building plans or money, and neither water nor electric service were available. There were little or no major sources of building materials and equipment in the area. About the only thing available in Haiti was cement and concrete blocks. Therefore, most of the material and equipment needed for the construction would have to be imported.

Various plans were formulated to address different segments of the building project and money to be raised by sponsoring different units of the radio station. Design plans for the facility were contributed by volunteers with design experience in their particular areas of expertise. All of this had to be incorporated into a final design plan and blueprints.

Next, we put together the construction schedule. Then we confronted what we thought was the biggest challenge: assembling work crews. We never had a reason to worry. God provided! People from roughly 18 states and a number of work teams from Canada volunteered their time and talents to the building project. More than 28,000 hours of labor were donated during the design and construction phases of the radio station project.

Purchasing materials and equipment and getting them to Haiti was a concern. I'd always been shy about bargaining and asking for donations, but God armed me for this task. When I visited a business, I took along a set of blueprints, which I used to sell the project and the need for the item I was soliciting. The number of positive responses amazed me.

Once the material was procured, it was trucked to Greenwood, loaded into containers, transported by truck and/or rail to Florida, then shipped to Haiti by boat – though it was anybody's guess when the boat would arrive in Cap Haitien. We finished getting the final roof section put in place a mere four hours before large crowds showed up for the dedication ceremony.

From the project's inception to its completion, Kay worked tirelessly on a variety of things: interior design, organizing women work crews, typing, etc. She was addicted to the project. And most importantly, she helped me keep my sanity.

I have been involved in a number of construction projects, but this one was memorable because of two talented men: Dave Shaferly and Gordon Wallace. These men were blessed with extensive construction knowledge, great people skills, and a lot of hands-on experience. They were the unsung heroes of the project.

Each mission trip has many memories, some dangerous, some meaningful, some humorous, and some life changing: getting finances into Russia, catching dengue fever in the Philippines, encountering armed gunmen in Colombia, having a six-year-old interpreter named Howie Young in Colombia, deciphering a set of Russian blueprints to rehab an existing sewage treatment plant in Ukraine, and seeing Velma Hardig swing her purse to fight off a band of gypsies attacking Warren. Velma won!

Of course, I will always treasure working with and praying with people in a multitude of countries. I feel so blessed to have been a part of the MFM story. Somewhere, somehow we all hope our involvement has made a difference in someone's life; being involved with MFM helps you know specific ways your life contributed while you were here on earth.

Jim Acheson (far right in cap) and team inspecting an irrigation system.

During one of my trips to Russia I was fortunate enough to attend a couple of Bible study groups consisting of Russian businessmen. Their knowledge of the Bible and the resulting dialogue was amazing and would put most of us to shame. These studies were taking place in Russia, of all places, which surprised me. I hope and trust the enthusiasm of the small groups there will be contagious and will ignite others there to become believers in Christ.

In 2000, Kay was diagnosed with cancer. We were devastated, but she was not a quitter. She still went on mission trips with me to Ukraine and Chile. She even made a couple of trips by herself to Haiti to work on several projects in the homes and the radio station. During our married life, we traveled to 30+ countries for business, pleasure, and mission work. In 2006, Kay died. I still vividly hear her parting words, "It was a great ride, wasn't it?" My world as I knew it was gone.

My dear friend Warren Hardig spoke at her funeral. In his description of her, he read Proverbs 31:20: "She extends her hand to the poor, and she stretches out her hands to the needy." Kay gave every part of herself to loving others and experiencing life with people. She will always be missed, but I know she is basking in the glory of the Lord, and I will see her again someday. I will forever be grateful for the opportunities Men for Missions provided us to serve the Lord.

The Tapestry of MFM

Warren Hardig

I have a file of precious treasures, including pictures of a multitude of MFMers. Many, if not all, of these men are dear friends I have prayed for, and they have prayed for me. They are part of an army of men who have given themselves away behind the scenes so more people, most of whom they have never met, could worship a living Savior. They have built schools for children they will never hear recite a poem, roads for people whose paths they will never cross, and churches for worshipers they will not meet this side of heaven.

Many of them have given money that, in the world's eyes, they could not afford to give. A service station owner gave away more than half his income (Charlie Smith's story is in *Motivated Men*); a blind man living on Social Security did ministry by faith (Chuck Merrill's story is in *Iron Sharpens Iron* and *Still Sharpening*); and a man whose life was so given to encouragement, he prayed over every single brick he laid at a youth camp in Brazil (Dale Larrance's story is in *Iron Sharpens Iron*).

Bill Evans (kneeling, forward facing) and team working on the Homes for Haiti project.

A typical work team improving the living standards of people in great need.

In my previous books, *Iron Sharpens Iron* and *Still Sharpening*, there are stories of a few of the men who have contributed to sharing the Gospel and have sharpened my life. It is my privilege to also acknowledge the wives of all the men of MFM, giving thanks to the multitude of wonderful, godly spouses who have so courageously supported us. Sometimes our wives traveled with us; other times we traveled on their prayers. Many of these women sacrificed by staying home and caring for their family so their husband would be free to minister as he felt God calling him.

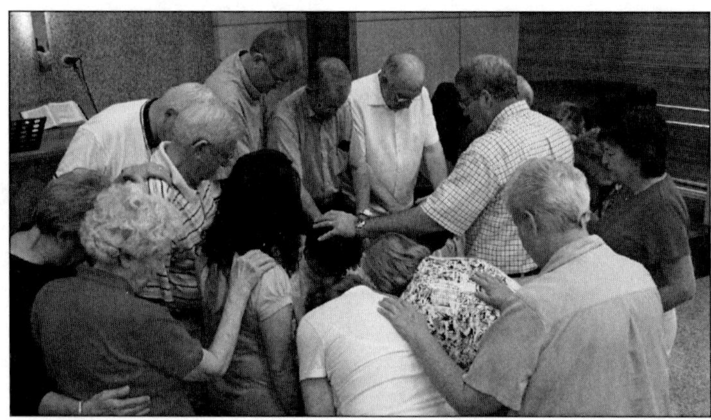

A common MFM scene, captured as men and women join their hearts in prayer for the nations (picture of prayer team taken in Taiwan.)

We thank God for every friendship, every person, and every praying heart, whether on the front line or behind the scenes. Each of these people are brightly colored threads in the amazing tapestry of Men for Missions. We deeply treasure these men and women, and the contributions they have made.

Epilogue

Thank you for reading this book, my humble attempt to share the stories of these great unsung men. I have been profoundly touched by many of them and hope you were, too.

In the early days of my church attendance I went to Blair Methodist Church, which stood at the intersection of two gravel roads in rural Illinois. Blair was well attended by our good friends and neighbors, and had three Sunday school classes. Unlike today, there was preaching every other Sunday. We were so remote that the preachers rotated among several churches, ours only getting a pastor to preach every other week.

The church was not only the spiritual hub, but was also the center of the community back in those days. Every year Blair hosted an evangelistic outreach, known as a revival. This was a time for us to invite unchurched friends and neighbors who might have heard about the young, enthusiastic preacher, but who might not want to be there for a Sunday morning service.

I will always remember the evening at one of those revivals when one of my best friends turned to me after the service and asked, "Warren, what did they want us to do when they kept asking us to come forward?"

My honest reply was, "I don't know."

How embarrassing it was for me to be the Sunday School superintendent and not know that the whole purpose of the revival was for people to come forward after hearing the message of salvation to ask Jesus to forgive their sins and be Lord of their lives. To provide the first step in a life dedicated to Christ.

It's God's desire that each person reading this book knows the answer to the question, "What will happen to me when I die?"

Do you?

By now you have read my testimony; it's your turn. Jesus wants *you* to know forgiveness and receive eternal life. Find a quiet place and talk to Him honestly about your needs. Don't try to manipulate Him or make a deal with Him. Simply ask Him for forgiveness and for Him to come into your life. He is leaning over the banister of heaven, waiting to hear from you. "For whoever will call on the name of the Lord will be saved" (Romans 10:13).

Be honest. Ask for His help. As you have read, it doesn't matter where you live, what color your skin is, or what language you speak; it is the message from your heart that matters.

If you haven't found peace in your heart, please don't waste another minute. Do it now. "Create in me a clean heart, O God, and renew a steadfast spirit within me" (Psalm 51:10).

If you have, God wants every believer to share his or her testimony. There is nothing in the world more precious than being forgiven of our sins. God's Word is full of His wonderful promises – the greatest wealth we believers have. We are commanded to share with those who do not yet know Him!

God wants everyone who has asked Him for forgiveness and received the assurance of salvation to tell others. Numerous scriptures tell this, and one of my favorites states it simply: "Come and hear, all who fear God, and I will tell of what He has done for my soul" (Psalm 66:16).

Who can you tell today?

Glossary of Terms

***ACTION* Magazine** – *ACTION* is the official publication of MFM, which tells the stories of how lives have been changed through this ministry.

AWANA – stands for "Approved Workmen Are Not Ashamed" (see 2 Timothy 2:15), a Bible-based program for youths ages 2-18.

Bike Teams – this type of team travels to different countries and rides bikes as a way to interact with people. It wasn't uncommon to have a lot of young people on these teams sharing Christ with indigenous people.

CoMission – The CoMission was a group of 82 Christian ministries that came together to teach Christian ethics and morality to the Russian people.

Doghouse – a small building usually covered with metal to eat meals, rest, change clothes, and store tools at the site of an oil well.

EvangeCube™ – is like a Rubik's cube that goes through the plan of salvation. There are different pictures depicting how we are separated from God, but we can be connected with Him again through salvation. It is an effective ministry tool for evangelism.

Flannel-Graph – a storytelling system that uses a board covered with flannel fabric, which usually rests on an easel and communicates a message.

"God Owns My Business" Initiative – Stanley Tam, our first MFMer, gave his business to the Lord years ago. In recent years, we had God Owns My Business dinners and seminars. At the dinners, often an evangelistic outreach, Stanley would give his testimony. At the seminars, we talked about God's principles for running a successful business and how to honor God with our businesses.

Holiness Camp Meeting – Different fundamental groups have established camps that often include cabins for overnight stays and a tabernacle for worship. Participants attend prayer meetings, fellowship with other Christians, and have opportunities to attend services led by several preachers throughout the day and evening. There is an emphasis on Christ being Lord and keys to holy living. It is a time set apart for spiritual refreshment.

Key Center English Center – created to teach the Japanese how to speak English. It has also been an effective evangelism tool.

MFM Council – These councils are groups of men who meet on a regular basis to pray for OMS missionaries. They often have an annual project they perform to help OMS. We recommend at least one member from the council goes on a ministry team every year, so the fire continues to burn from within.

MFMI – Men for Missions was started in 1954. International was added to our name because there was already a different group called Men for Missions that was started in 1952 in Chicago by Harry Conn. We have been MFMI until recently, when we became Men for Missions Global (MFMG).

Moscow Evangelical Christian Seminary – a seminary started by OMS in the 1990s to train the indigenous people how to be effective pastors and missionaries. Currently over 700 students participate in class and online.

Navigators Topical Memory System – an effective way to learn key verses of the Bible. There is often a small, portable box of small cards with Scripture verses on them. You are encouraged to memorize those Scriptures to help with discipline; it is the perfect launching point to begin hiding God's word in your heart.

Operation Saturation – was started in the early 2000s. MFM raised money and materials to build the new broadcast center for Radio 4VEH.

Radio 4VEH – MFM purchased this ministry years ago. This station shares farming information, news and life education. It also presents the Gospel and Christian education in English, Spanish, and Creole across the islands of the Caribbean.

Sanctified/Sanctification – the second work of grace, subsequent to being born again, in which a person yields his life totally to Jesus Christ.

Teacher's Conference – These convocations were designed to tell the teachers in Russia about Jesus Christ. We also taught Christian ethics and morality from a Biblical perspective.

Tokyo Bible Seminary – an OMS seminary in Tokyo where we train our pastors.

Youth Camp on Ōshima Island – a youth camp that MFM built many years ago in the south of Japan. Youth camps have provided great ministry opportunities for us.

Velma, Clance LaTurner, Warren

Written Materials

Any book referred to in this book written by Gene Bertolet (*Warfare Prayer Manual*s), Dwight Ferguson (*Motivated Men*), Stanley Tam (*God Owns my Business*), or Warren Hardig (*Iron Sharpens Iron* and *Still Sharpening*) can be obtained by reaching out to One Mission Society, 317-888-3333, or via e-mail at info@onemissionsociety.org